IN EVE'S ATTIRE

Also by Delphine Horvilleur in English translation

Anti-Semitism Revisited

DELPHINE HORVILLEUR

IN EVE'S ATTIRE

Modesty, Judaism and the Female Body

Translated from the French by
Ruth Diver

MACLEHOSE PRESS
QUERCUS · LONDON

First published in the French language as *En tenue d'Ève*
by Éditions Grasset & Fasquelle, 2013
First published in Great Britain in 2022 by

MacLehose Press
An imprint of Quercus Publishing Ltd
Carmelite House
50 Victoria Embankment
London EC4Y 0DZ

An Hachette UK company

The authorised representative in the EEA is Hachette Ireland, 8 Castlecourt
Centre, Dublin 15, D15 XTP3, Ireland (email: info@hbgi.ie)

ISBN (Hardback) 978 1 52940 477 7
ISBN (Ebook) 978 1 52940 478 4

This book is a work of fiction. Names, characters, businesses,
organisations, places and events are either the product of the author's
imagination or are used fictitiously. Any resemblance to actual persons,
living or dead, events or locales is entirely coincidental.

All URLs provided in footnotes and Bibliography were correct at
the time of going to press.

Designed and typeset in Haarlemmer by Libanus Press Ltd
Printed and bound in Great Britain by Clays Ltd, Elcograf S.p.A.

The world only exists because of the breath
of children engaged in Torah study.

(Talmud)

For my children
Samuel, Ella and Alma
So they build a world from constant reading.

Wrap yourself in this skin, leave the palace, and walk
so long as you can find ground to carry you: when one
sacrifices everything to virtue the gods know
how to mete out reward.

(Charles Perrault, "Donkey-Skin")

CONTENTS

Translator's Note

Quotations from Jewish texts are from Sefaria.org, unless otherwise indicated. Those from the New Testament are given in the King James Version. All unattributed translations of other sources are my own.

Introduction

For decades now, we have been living in a culture where we are supposed to have "nothing to hide" – an era of exhibitionism, in which there are hardly any constraints imposed on our desire to see and be seen. Visibility and transparency are praised as manifestations of individual freedom. In political life and personal relationships, transparency is perceived as an assurance of morality, a promise of authenticity and sincerity. Conversely, any lack of transparency is seen as suspicious behaviour or an admission of guilt. In the name of visibility, intimacy is often thwarted and the boundaries between public and private life become blurred.

What does modesty even mean, in the era of Facebook and reality TV? Some see it as an old-fashioned concept – an anachronistic, noxious leftover of a bygone era. Others, however, think modesty is something that should be rehabilitated in a society that exposes far too much. In the last few years, the most virulent discourse in favour of enforcing norms of modesty has come from religious spokespersons, in particular from the defenders of the Muslim veil in France.

According to them, the obscenity of Western society presents such a threat to women and their dignity that it justifies measures encouraging them to cover themselves.

The characteristic feature of this fundamentalist rhetoric is its claim that these requirements for modest dress and behaviour are for women's benefit, even though its goal is often to make them less visible. It seeks to eliminate women from public space "for their own good", and to eradicate the desire that women provoke.

There is something obscene in this obsession with the extinction of desire, in the way that it completely reduces women to the temptation their bodies represent. The modesty imposed by religious traditions is thus often paradoxical: it claims to be about decency, while running the risk of obscenity. It makes all of a woman's body taboo, as if every part of it was a sexual organ that must be kept hidden at all times in public spaces. All women are reduced to a status where they have no face, and thus no individuality: they can express nothing except their gendered nature.

By way of symmetry, men also find themselves amputated of a part of their anatomy: their eyelids. A man is nothing but eyes or, more exactly, is what Fethi Benslama calls a "man-pupil",[1] a being incapable of restraining his sight or even blinking, one who is forced to "leer". Lacking

1 "Le voile de l'Islam" (The veil of Islam), *Contretemps*, 2/3 (1997), pp. 99–111.

a membrane to obstruct his vision, he demands that women should cover themselves with the eyelid-veil of which he is denuded. Women without faces and men without eyelids: these excessive attempts to protect the body lead to symbolic amputations in both sexes.

This is why it is now necessary for religious voices from all traditions to revisit the notions of modesty that lie at the heart of the sacred texts. Modesty cannot consist of an obsessional veiling of the bodies of others. It must be about accepting that no-one can be entirely visible in their nakedness. No-one can ever unveil themselves completely. Something in them always escapes us, for they cannot be reduced to the desire they arouse in us, nor to the images of them that a sacred text might carry.

What is true for humans is true for texts as well. The only modest reading of scripture is one which affirms that the text has not yet been revealed completely or laid bare by past readings and readers. When interpretation fixes texts, it profanes them. Are they then still sacred? They can only remain so if we accept that they have more to show and more to say.

This is the only way for us to set out on our journey through the texts. While this study specifically considers Jewish sources, an exploration like this one cannot be exclusively about Judaism. No religious tradition has the monopoly on immodest readings. It is up to all traditions to take up the work required to find a way out of the obscene interpretations that some of their readers or leaders often lock themselves into.

CHAPTER ONE

No Woman's Land

Bus number 451: the Ashdod–Jerusalem route.

Tanya Rosenblit, a young woman aged twenty-eight, boards a vehicle belonging to Egged, the public transport company. She sits at the front of the bus, just behind the driver, so he can tell her which stop to get off at. A man then boards the bus and asks her to move and sit at the back with the other women. On this so-called "kosher" route, the Haredim or ultra-orthodox Jews try to impose strict segregation between men and women. Such segregation is illegal in Israel, but some bus companies tolerate it in practice. Not Tanya Rosenblit. The young woman refuses to move, and the conversation quickly becomes heated. The man holds the doors open to prevent the bus from leaving, but the young woman does not give way. In the end she stays in her seat for the whole trip to Jerusalem. Within a few hours, the news is relayed over social media networks, then by the press, making this young Israeli woman a new Rosa Parks, an icon of the opposition to discrimination.

*

It is December 16, 2011. Starting with this incident, and in the space of a few weeks, several events seem to indicate a trend emerging in the ultra-orthodox religious world: the increasing exclusion of women from public spaces. The Israeli press finds a new term for this concept, this attempt to keep women at a distance from the public sphere or collective space: *hadarat nashim* (the exclusion of women).

In some ultra-orthodox neighbourhoods in Israel, signage encouraging physical distancing between men and women then starts to proliferate in the streets. "Woman, do not linger here!" "Change footpaths!" The parliament, the government and the Israeli people in their vast majority cry scandal. The prime minister, Benjamin Netanyahu, and the president of the State of Israel, Shimon Peres, firmly denounce this derailment: it is not acceptable that a small extremist group should threaten the egalitarian foundation and liberal values of Israeli society.

And yet, in Jerusalem, as a result of pressure from ultra-orthodox communities, women's faces disappear from many advertising posters in the city. Whether in images or in the flesh, women vanish, having been encouraged to stay away and not disturb the men. This distancing is always insisted upon in the name of a religious value: *tzniut*, Hebrew for "modesty".

A happy (wo)man is a hidden (wo)man

Tzniut is a religious concept that originally prescribed the behaviour to be adopted in order to avoid any promiscuous situations, to preserve oneself from any kind of debauchery, and to maintain a humble and discreet attitude in all circumstances.

As it is described in traditional Jewish literature, *tzniut* in theory applies to men as much as women. In daily experience, though, this "modesty" requires only women to practise restraint and distance. The requirement for modesty in men, at any rate, does not seem to involve the same diligence as for women. For years now, there has been a flourishing internet market for modest clothing for practising women, while press articles or advertising guarantee the social and even sexual happiness of couples who observe the principles of modesty. A Jewish marriage guidance site affirms: "No sexuality can be satisfying on every level if notions of sanctity and modesty are not respected."[2]

But what danger does a woman's physical presence and her too obvious visibility present to men? The ultra-orthodox position insists that female exposure represents a double threat. First of all, men run the risk of losing control, being

2   "Sexualité féminine et judaïsme – Se préparer à l'intimité", Ecoute juive, www.ecoute-juive.com/nidah-sexualite-et-plaisir-femme-et-thora.php.

led astray and turned from the straight and narrow path. But women's dignity itself is also seen as being in peril. Women need to be protected from themselves, to be brought back to their true calling or their essence: being veiled.

In the Jewish tradition, women's modesty is frequently associated with a biblical verse that is said to prescribe it: "The treasure of the king's daughter is inside" (Psalm 45:14–15[3]). Without any context, this sentence is far from explicit. Originally, it described the material riches of a sovereign's heiress as a treasure that should be kept hidden. But the traditional rabbinical interpretation uses this sentence to justify the practice of keeping every woman inside – both inside herself and inside her home – to make her an "indoor woman" and to prevent what is feminine from slipping out of the domestic sphere. The "king's daughter" is "honoured" by being distanced from the outside world. This relegation guarantees the permanent exclusion of the female gender from public space, where it would present a danger – for men as well as for the social order. Rabbi Zvi Thau, a perfect contemporary advocate of that interpretation and one of the leaders of Orthodox Judaism in Israel, declared in July 2012 that "the home is the best place for a woman to be happy, and not the social sphere. It is at home, away from the agitation [of the world] that a woman can live her life in full."[4]

3 Author's translation.
4 *Haaretz*, July 31, 2012.

When a woman leaves her home, as soon as she ventures outside, she must cover her body as well as anything extending beyond it – in particular her head and hair, if she is married – in order not to provoke men, who would be "beside themselves" at the sight of such a spectacle. The requirement for modesty extends to everything emanating from a woman, not just her hair, skin or clothing, but also her voice. In the Talmud, a sage asserts that "a woman's voice is considered nakedness" (Babylon Talmud, Berkhot treatise 24a.[5]). Some people would like to turn this personal opinion into an undisputable law. According to them, the female voice, whether singing or in some circumstances even spoken, constitutes an indecency, an exhibition that should be contained or veiled in public spaces.

"Women's voices are considered nakedness"

Within a few weeks of the incident on the bus, other pillars of social integration are shaken by further sectarian upheavals, among them one of the emblematic centres of gender equality: the army.

At about the same time as Tanya Rosenblit raises her voice and refuses to leave her seat, IDF soldiers refuse to stay in theirs and leave in the middle of a military ceremony,

5 Author's translation.

because women's singing is imposed upon them during the celebrations. The Israeli army, known for including women in its troops from its very beginnings, is suddenly shaken by a strange demand from a local rabbi. Elyakim Levanon, the head of a yeshiva (a Talmudic school) that sends its students to serve in the army, calls on all practising soldiers in service to leave any ceremony where there are women singing. He bases this call on the same mysterious passage in the Talmud asserting that "a woman's voice is considered nakedness" and recommends that his students boycott any event where women's singing voices are heard, "even at the peril of their lives".[6] The military chiefs of staff do not give way, and firmly condemn all calls for segregation, but the year 2012 offers a surprising rabbinical version of the sirens luring the sailors with their song in the *Odyssey*.

Is this an extreme, marginal, unrepresentative interpretation, or is it a faithful reading of the sources? Other rabbinical authorities, without calling on men to pay with their lives, relay this proscription of hearing a woman singing. In France, the nakedness that a female singer constitutes is regularly invoked by representatives of Judaism: in March 2010, for example, the Chief Rabbi of Paris, David Messas, attempted to stop the singer Talila from performing in a suburban community centre on the outskirts of Paris, in the name

6 *Haaretz*, January 16, 2012.

of that same prohibition, before eventually backing down.[7]

As accounts of segregation between men and women multiply, some commentators professing more modern views within that same orthodox world strive to emphasise the marginal nature of these events in the Jewish community.

Several leading religious figures argue that this fundamentalist drift is attributable only to small minority groups and is not representative of ultra-orthodoxy, and that it is not in any way the legitimate legacy of Jewish readings of the scriptures. In an interview given to the French Press Association on January 7, 2012, the Chief Rabbi of France, Gilles Bernheim, describes these "ultra-orthodox" groups, who receive considerable media coverage as a "tiny minority", while also deploring the "silence of some rabbis [which] leaves the way open to extremists".[8]

Here and there, calls for a more open interpretation can be heard, and counteroffensives are even being organised. In the midst of the controversy, the Orthodox rabbi Menachem Froman invites both male and female musicians to perform in his synagogue. Questioned on issues of tolerance and the presence of women in his place of worship, he declares: "There are secular values that are important to me, and the

7 *Le Monde*, March 5, 2010.
8 "Le silence des rabbins" (The silence of the rabbis), *Les Dernières Nouvelles d'Alsace*, 11 January 2012, https://www.dna.fr/religions/2012/01/11/le-silence-des-rabbins.

place of women in modern society is, in my eyes, closer to the divine than it was in traditional society." He adds: "A woman cannot be reduced to the opportunity for temptation that she constitutes."[9]

At the heart of these polemics is a confrontation between different views that are not necessarily reconcilable. Must modernity trample on tradition, or can it in fact also be a vehicle for the sacred? How can one determine whether an interpretation is legitimate, anachronistic or corrupted?

The all-genital woman

What do these recent events all have in common? The recurring calls for exclusion and segregation are all based on scripture, and claim to be legitimate and traditional inter-pretations, based on sacred sources of which they offer the only reliable readings.

Neither visible nor audible, women are kept at a distance from the public sphere. Their bodies, and, by metonymy, any of their bodily parts or attributes, come to be considered as exposed nakedness, capable of arousing men's desire. This gives rise to a religious rhetoric that hypersexualises women, reducing them to only what their bodies might catalyse in men.

9 *Haaretz*, December 16, 2011.

In the name of modesty, any visible or audible surface is rendered potentially obscene. For women, the zone of immodest exposure covers the entire body, including hidden anatomical elements like their vocal cords. Their bodies are thus more naked than men's, for they are naked on the inside as well as on the outside, exposed even when they are covered. What for men carries speech and translates thought – the voice – is considered a sexual characteristic in women. What is feminine is indecent, not only when female genital organs are exposed, but also when the eroticised head is.

Is this obsession a pathology of a tiny religious group or is it legitimised by tradition? Does sexual obsession have a textual origin? Does the interpretation of texts necessarily impel us to ascribe to women the responsibility for the irrepressible desire they arouse?

Covered heads

The hyper-sexualisation of women's bodies is specific neither to the Jewish tradition nor to the religious world more generally. In his painting titled *The Rape*, René Magritte depicts the face of a woman whose head is replaced or symbolised by sexual organs. The eyes are breasts, the mouth a mons pubis. The artist seems to suggest that violence against women is often due to the transformation of their face into a genital zone, an object of desire. In this painting, just like in some kinds of religious fundamentalism, a flagrant inequality between the sexes is expressed: whereas a man's voice is a tool for public expression, a woman's voice is only a tool for "pubic" expression.

In their book *Off With Her Head! The Denial of Women's Identity in Myth, Religion and Culture*, Howard Eilberg-Schwartz and Wendy Doniger assert that the insistence on veiling women in many cultures is born precisely from the eroticisation of their face and head. Getting rid of the head by covering it constitutes a symbolic decapitation, which conceals the principal marker of personal autonomy and individual differentiation.

Veiling women, their face or their hair is a phenomenon that is common to several religions and cultures. The Islamic veil is the most prominent expression of this practice, and no doubt the most controversial one in the last few years. But the phenomenon is, or has been, present in other civilisations, in both East and West. Roman culture provides an example of this: the origin of the word "nubile", meaning "of marriageable age", is the Latin *nubere*, which literally means "to veil oneself" (from *nubes*, "mist"). In ancient Greece, marriage was associated with an act of covering one's head. At the heart of the wedding ceremony was a ritual called *anakalupteria*: the moment when the bride temporarily showed her face, before covering it again.

Veiling the face of a bride seems, in many cultures, to mark the change in her status from unmarried to married. This association is found in the Jewish wedding ceremony, which traditionally starts with an uncovering/recovering. The bridegroom approaches the bride, observes her face, then covers it with a veil. From that precise moment on, in the most orthodox Jewish communities, the woman covers her head and only reveals her hair in private to her husband.

In the writings of the Christian world, the apostle Paul also defends the veil. According to him, it is through this act of covering oneself that the difference between the sexes is made conspicuously manifest. In the First Epistle to the Corinthians, he writes that men should be unveiled and women veiled because "Every man praying or prophesying, having his head covered, dishonoureth his head. But every woman that prayeth or prophesieth with her head uncovered dishonoureth her head" (1 Corinthians 11:4–5). According to the apostle, this is how the woman affirms that she is under the authority of her husband. Because woman was created for man, and not the other way around, she must carry on her head a sign of submission.

As a counterpoint to Paul's theory, in Judaism, covering the head is not reserved for women. Practising men wear the kippah. When this tradition arose is not known precisely; it does not appear in ancient texts, but seems to have become normative in the Middle Ages. This male head covering also expresses a form of submission or, more accurately, the recognition that a transcendent authority exists, under which man is humbly placed.

Men and women thus don't cover their heads for the same reasons in Judaism: the former are encouraged to mark the presence of transcendence in all circumstances from early childhood onwards, whereas the latter only cover themselves when they are married, and only in public. Whereas veils, hats or wigs can symbolise a form of submission, they are mostly a social marker that informs others of the non-availability of the covered woman.[10] The head covering is thus worn to regulate the temptation of other men.

We must insist on the fact that desire itself is not what is condemned in this view: an unmarried woman can leave her head uncovered, because she can be legally desired. The problem is not the arousal of a man's desire, but the arousal of a forbidden desire, which might lead him to covet another man's "possession". It is thus not an issue of temptation but of property. The veil, here, must act as a brake on the male libido: its purpose is to domesticate the woman and the desire she arouses, in the name of the social order.

10 According to Rabbi Louis Epstein, Jewish women cover themselves primarily to signal that they are the exclusive property of a man. See Louis M. Epstein, *Sex Laws and Customs in Judaism* (Hoboken, NJ: Ktav Publishing House, 1968).

Woman: hero or zero

The model "indoor" or "domesticated" woman is not the one who comes to life in the pages of the Bible. Many biblical heroines distinguish themselves, on the contrary, by their capacity to play a public and political role. Several are described as prophetesses, whose words, acts and songs provide guidance to the people. Among them, one could mention Esther, Miriam, Deborah, Ruth and Tamar, or the young shepherdess of the Song of Songs who sings of her desire in an apologia of free femininity and a non-domesticated loving relationship.

But the Jewish and Christian literature published in the first centuries CE shows a radical change of tone with regard to women. The rabbinical writings and those of the first Christians seem to impose a new orientation in the approach to women and femininity, no doubt under the influence of the Greco-Roman world.

Women are suddenly described in other terms. Now, these troublemakers must "wear the dunce's hat", as those responsible for the original transgression and human decadence. Jews and Christians also start advising men to avoid the company of women and anything that is essentially female, which is seen as noxious in its very nature.

Thus Philo of Alexandria, a Jew living in a Hellenised world, writes in the first century that woman "is a selfish creature, excessively jealous and adept at beguiling the morals of her husband and seducing him by her continued impostures".[11] In his *Antiquitates Judaicae*, the Roman historian Josephus declares a few decades later that women constitute a danger for the community of men and that letting women into a group opens the way for dissension.

Some Jewish laws established at that time do institute a precursory status for women and a form of social protection: the marriage contract defined by the Talmud, for example, endows the wife with certain rights during the marriage and in case of divorce. However, Jewish literature from the beginning of the Common Era reflects the time it was written in, and therefore encourages its male readers to master or domesticate women. The rights and protection from which a woman might benefit are contingent on her status as a wife and mother. She can enjoy them only as long as she accepts her interior status, in other words, being confined to her home. Ben Sira, a Jewish author from the second century BCE, writes that "a daughter is a treasure that keeps her father wakeful, and worry over her drives away rest [...] See that there is no lattice in her room, no place that overlooks the approaches to the house" (Ben Sira, 42:9–11). A woman is a precious possession to be hidden away for her own good, and for that of her family and society. The

11 Philo, *Hypothetica* 11.14, in *Philo Volume IX*, tr. F. H. Colson, Loeb Classical Library 363 (Cambridge: Harvard University Press, 1941), p. 443.

role she is assigned is that of an interior presence (and preferably with no window to the outside), in the service of a man: "Wives must be in servitude to their husband, a servitude not imposed by violent ill-treatment but promoting obedience in all things," writes Philo.[12] The woman is clearly given the status of a dependant in relation to another person. She is a "zero", in the sense of "less than one": an individual with no autonomy, whose integrity exists only insofar as she is subject to the authority of the father or husband to whom she is submitted.

The woman who is not submitted, on the other hand, is given revealing names. She is sometimes called a *yatzanit*, literally "the one who goes out", the extrovert, the debauched one. In other instances, she is called *mufkeret*; this adjective, which originally described an abandoned, uncultivated, ownerless piece of land, and by extension was also the definition of a prostitute, is also used to qualify a woman who is not under the ascendancy and control of a man. With no master or owner, her dignity is threatened, and with it, social peace.

Kept at home, women are also kept at a distance from the sites of power. The centre of power, for the rabbis, is not the street or the forum, but a space that is the ultimate "no woman's land": the yeshiva, the house of study. The leader

12 *Hypothetica* 7.3, ibid., p. 425.

of the community is first and foremost a scholar: he exerts his power through knowledge, reading and interpretation, in other words, with his voice.

From Yentl to the present day

The yeshiva is traditionally a world of men who read and talk, a world full of the hubbub of study. It is therefore a world in which women, silent and hidden, have no part, a space in which they symbolise absolute marginality. This is the origin of the literary myth of Yentl, so wonderfully portrayed in Isaac Bashevis Singer's short story[13] and incarnated in a film by Barbra Streisand. In this story, the young Yentl, who is passionate about study and educated by her father in the love of scripture, disguises herself as a man to gain access to the yeshiva. There she meets and falls in love with Avigdor, who believes her to be a young male student named Anshel, with whom he enthusiastically plunges into the pages of books and Talmudic debate. When she finally reveals her identity to him, he cannot believe that she dared to breach those prohibitions. To dress and study like a man is a double travesty. If not for those transgressions, he tells her, "we could have been married". "But I want to

13 "Yentl the Yeshiva Boy", *The Collected Stories of Isaac Bashevis Singer*, tr. Marion Magid and Elizabeth Pollet (London: Jonathan Cape, 1982).

study the Gemara and Commentaries with you, not darn your socks," Yentl responds.[14]

"What would it be like if a woman studied with us?" This rhetorical question is asked by rabbis in other foundational stories, including in the Talmud, where one finds a woman called Beruriah, who was said to be more erudite than all the men around her. But every time the scholars consider such a situation, they point to it as a threat to the system of the house of study. As if the very survival of the political and social organisation that is the yeshiva depended on the exclusion of women. As if its structure might be toppled by the admission of women and the consequent confusion of genders.

Playing on the well-known qualifier, "the people of the Book", Armand Abécassis describes the Jews as "the people of the interpretation of the book". But in fact, for millennia, only half of "the people" were invited to take part in this sacred exercise of interpretation and reading. Times have changed, and our generation is seeing a revolution.

Over the last few decades, women have taken up study and entered through the doors of a few yeshivot.[15] In Germany in the 1930s, Regina Jonas became the first female rabbi. In the United States, starting in the 1970s, the rabbinate has been feminised, as houses of study have

14 Ibid., p. 165.
15 Plural of yeshiva.

opened their doors to women. This is the case in the liberal Jewish world, of course, but also in the traditionalist world. Yeshivot have developed where women study the Talmud, alone or with men, such as the Drisha Institute in New York, or Matan, in Jerusalem. In 2009, Sarah Hurvitz became the first woman to have attained the title of rabba (the feminine form of "rabbi") in an orthodox seminary. Needless to say, her ordination is not universally recognised, notably not by the consistorial voices of French Judaism. As I was writing this, there were only two of us female rabbis in France, and we officiated in liberal congregations. Our numbers have now grown to five. Our legitimacy is not presently recognised by the consistory, even if several million Jews throughout the world are affiliated with progressive movements in Judaism.

The Chief Rabbi of France, at the start of 2011 (perhaps in reaction to episodes of segregation in Israel), affirmed his wish to develop and promote women's religious education. A "women's Jewish studies" circle opened its doors at the Grand Synagogue of Paris in October 2012. It is exclusively for women.

In the religious world more widely, we now urgently have to rehabilitate women's voices, in dialogue with the sacred texts and with men. This evolution will be possible only if women's bodies are no longer perceived as exposed nakedness.

CHAPTER TWO

Preamble to a Jewish Reading . . .
Or How to Become a "Text Maniac"

In an interview in 1998 with the French newspaper *Libéra-tion*, Rabbi Marc-Alain Ouaknin, a renowned exegete of Jewish sources, defined himself as a "text maniac".[16] This syndrome might be something experienced by all inter-preters of Jewish sources: a passion for the text and its commentary.

When the Temple in Jerusalem was destroyed in 70 CE, a small group of scholars led a religious revolution that would enable the transition from a Judaism of priests and prophets, of sacrifices and pilgrimages, to a Judaism of rabbis and sages, of prayers and synagogues. Deprived of the geograph-ical centre that was the only place where worship had been conducted, these rabbis created and imposed a new leading class, with different rituals. From that point onwards, the divine was approached through the text, and not through the intermediary of sacrificed animals. It was the book, and its interpretation, that became the privileged space for the

16 *Libération*, June 22, 1998.

encounter with the sacred, and no longer the steps of the Temple. Time spent reading became a space for worship. The culture of the texts and their interpretation is undoubtedly, in its own way, the reconstructed Temple of rabbinic Judaism.

Through this revolution, the Jews thus became the people of the interpretation of the Book, or more accurately, of the *interpretations* of the Book. The literature of the commentaries is composed of many different exegeses: legal, narrative, mystical . . . This richness leads to an explosion of the text into a multitude of possible readings and meanings, of intersecting significations. The page of the Talmud is the best ambassador for this polysemy. The text is presented visually: surrounding its first transposition into writing are criss-crossing contrary opinions, a dialogue between authorities of different epochs commenting on a single verse or text. These commentators, often living in different times and places, meet on the page and allow one mind to fertilise another. A page of the Talmud is the literary illustration of the art of not reaching agreement or, as the French expression has it, not "falling into agreement", which suggests that conciliation is indeed a fall. How, then, can we not consider the debating of ideas, or disagreement, to be anything other than an elevation? In the Jewish tradition at least, open debate, which is held up as a value in itself, has a name: *machloket*, which literally means "cut" or "scission". This scission of opinions and words reflects the Talmudic tradition, the elevation to an art form of the act of cutting the text into numerous reading fragments.

> Just as this hammer breaks a stone into several fragments, so too, one verse is stated by God and from it emerge several explanations. [Babylon Talmud, Sanhedrin 34a]

For the rabbis of the Talmud, the biblical text is akin to a petrified mineral structure, a fixed rock, waiting only for a blow from the stonecutter, its interpreter. Once the rock has exploded, each split provides a new reading, a precious glint of possible meaning.

The text never says one single thing, or rather, it never says it once and for all: that is the underlying principle of rabbinic interpretation. The characters will not speak their last words until they meet their last readers.

How, then, can we know whether a new reading is legitimate and faithful? How can we tell the difference between the discovery of a hidden meaning by a new reader and pure invention? The sages, conscious that a text can become whatever anyone makes it say or allows it to say, had strived to ensure that this new reader would not be just anybody, but a recognised authority, or someone who might have a claim to be one, who might be inscribed as a link in the chain of interpretations and interpreters.

Hebrew, the language of tailors

Although the revolution that elevated divergence to a value to be upheld was crucial, this culture of multiple interpretations can be seen as inherent in the very structure of the Hebrew language and its grammar. Hebrew is a language constructed around roots that appear in a multitude of signifiers. By the simple addition of vowels, suffixes or prefixes, three letters give birth to many words, which are linked by a meaning that is not always obvious.

Let us take three Hebrew letters as an example: *dalet* (ד), *vet* (ב) and *resh* (ר), respectively pronounced as "D", "V" and "R". The root formed from these three letters gives birth to words as varied as *DaVaR* – "speech", *DeVeR* – "plague", *DeVoRa* – "bee". The meanings of these three words don't appear to have anything in common, but they are in fact vehicles for a common idea, that of propagation. The bee flying from flower to flower allows for the diffusion of pollen and the propagation of seed. The plague is the evil of contamination par excellence in biblical thinking, whose spread escapes us. Speech is the method of propagating messages, from one being to another.

To explore a root by engaging the words it creates in dialogue with each other is to visit the universe of Hebraic thought, its mental structure and its wisdom. From three letters, Hebrew builds a universe of intersecting meanings, woven into each other and connected far beyond the context of their specific usage.

In the Bible, writing is only consonantal. It is up to the readers to place both the vowels and the punctuation. Up to them, in their reading, to choose between "speech", "plague" or "bee". They are the ones who, from the context and their own intuition, give a firm meaning to an open text that tolerates multiple readings.

Rabbinical interpretation traditionally plays with this polysemy of the language, and always invites us to graft a new meaning onto an original verse that is treated like a raw material that must be worked, a pattern that must be sewn together. The verse is stark naked, and the reader must dress it.

This is what Stéphane Zagdanski expresses when he writes that

> rabbis experienced the text as a texture, and reading as sewing, a pulsatile work of cutting and suturing, ceaselessly linking the fibres of the book (letters, words, verses, expressions, opinions, errors, repetitions, interpolations, commentary, interpretations of

commentary, varied traditions and heresies) to each other and to what is beyond them, to the interior invention of their transmission. The rabbis never stopped cutting, snipping, slicing into this living material passed from generation to generation, weaving their incomparable masterpiece of intellectual fervour, just as others, in the same era, were chiselling their first cathedrals.[17]

It is troubling to realise to what extent, throughout Jewish history, sewing has been perceived as a Jewish activity. As tailors, furriers or merchants, the Jews often specialised in trades to do with cloth and its handling. It goes without saying that this choice of occupation, for many Jews, was often imposed by their history of peregrinations and wanderings, privations and prohibitions. Easily transportable, sewing is the craft practised by those who must be ready to leave everything behind and take to the road, with only a few pieces of fabric, scissors, thread and patterns. Sewing is the ultimate activity, involving recycling, travel and transitions: what was originally used for one thing is later used for another, what was worn here will be worn there, or elsewhere, or differently.

Ashkenazic Jewish humour claims this transgenerational

17   Stéphane Zagdanski, *L'Impureté de Dieu* (The impurity of God) (Paris: Éditions du Félin, 1991), p. 14.

love of "shmattology", the science of *shmattes*, as its own. *Shmattes* is a word that signifies "rag" in Yiddish, or "low-quality cloth". To be "in shmattes" is to work in textiles in general, of good or bad quality – to be in the rag trade. There are countless jokes that play on this Jewish love of clothing: "My son, now that you have graduated from Harvard and the École Polytechnique, you'll need to choose between tailoring for men and tailoring for women."

But the attachment to clothing in Judaism is perhaps also the reflection of a more profound passion, which reveals the essence of the spirit of an ancestral tradition, a religion of text and textile.

What if approaching the text as one approaches a textile was truly a Jewish art?

Alterations to the text

In French and English, the words "text" and "textile" derive from the same etymological root. Text, texture, textile, tissue . . . all these words share an Indo-European root, inherited by the Latin *textus*, which expresses the action of assembling, of constructing items made from intersecting materials. This link between text and cloth can be found in a number of French and English expressions: a "thread" can be the plot of a story as well as a weaver's material, the elements of that plot are sometimes only roughly "stitched together". This lexical closeness exists in many languages. In English, "spinning a yarn" is used for stories as well as for thread.

Hebrew similarly plays with this interweaving of worlds, of the tasks of interpretation and of tailoring. Each book of the Talmud is called a *masekhet*, a "treatise". When you look up the word in a Biblical Hebrew dictionary, you find that *masekhet* originally meant the warp and weft of the loom, where the threads of the *shmattes* are interwoven. Jewish law and the Talmud, its primary commentary, are thus written on a weaver's loom.[18]

All stories are sewn together from a fabric of interwoven threads. In Jewish thought, this assertion can most obviously be applied to the most pre-eminent "text" of all, that of divine revelation. The Bible, for the Jews, is a work of haute couture, one with a divine pattern: the central text, the primary fabric of the written Torah, is interwoven with commentaries, interpretations and tales, like so many incisions and alterations.

18 Hebrew has numerous words whose etymology interweaves both "story" and "sewing". The word for cloth, *bad*, also means to invent, to tell tall tales. Science fiction is called *mada bidioni*, or literally "the science of cloth". See Francine Kaufmann's essay "Introduction au tissu et au vêtement dans la Bible et le Judaïsme" (Introduction to cloth and clothing in the Bible and Judaism), in *Shmattès. La mémoire par le rebut* (Shmattes: memory from scraps), ed. Céline Masson (Limoges: Éditions Lambert-Lucas, 2007), pp. 207–20.

Each generation continues the work of sewing together the text it has inherited, adding stitches to the original, padding out the reading and making alterations to it to ensure it will be handed down to the next generation. On a page of the Talmud, a Bible verse is commented on by a rabbi, then by another sage, then another. Each generation must top-stitch the preceding commentary, and pursue a conversation embroidered over the centuries. Traditional Jewish literature is the embodiment of "shmattology".

Marcel Proust followed the same process in *In Search of Lost Time*, defining his literary enterprise in the following terms: "Pinning here and there an additional page, I should construct my book, I dare not say ambitiously like a cathedral, but quite simply like a dress."[19]

No reading in the nude!

Jewish interpretation has a reputation for splitting hairs, or as the French say, "splitting hairs into four". Anecdotally, four is a number that is pertinent to rabbinical exegesis. According to some traditional texts, four levels of reading exist for each verse, along with four interpretative universes.

19 Marcel Proust, *In Search of Lost Time, Vol. 6: Time Regained*, tr. Andreas Mayor and Terence Kilmartin, rev. D. J. Enright (New York: Modern Library, 1981).

The first level, or literal sense, is called Peshat, the second is Remez, the allusive sense. Then there is Derash, the allegorical sense, and finally Sod, the hidden meaning of the text.

The order of these terms is meaningful in itself: the acrostic formed by the four initials of these words, P-R-D-S, forms the word *pardes*, Hebrew for "orchard". This word shares the etymology of another one that has migrated into French and English: "paradise". To interpret a term, to navigate between different levels of reading, is to travel towards the Garden of Eden, a paradise of the senses. Reading is the ultimate sensual experience.

In order to understand the Jewish reading of the Bible, it is essential to realise that a literal reading is not really part of it. A verse never simply means what it appears to mean and can never be reduced to its explicit meaning.

Even the first level of interpretation, Peshat, which we sometimes translate as the "obvious meaning", is not what might be conventionally called the "literal meaning". Let us take one of the most famous verses of the Bible as an example, the law of retaliation or *lex talionis* and principle of retributive justice: "An eye for an eye, a tooth for a tooth." The meaning of this verse appears on first reading to have nothing ambiguous about it. The punishment inflicted is similar to the harm caused. However, the so-called literal rabbinical reading of this verse never considers removing an eye from the person who might have torn out their neighbour's, but rather suggests that the loss of an eye should be compensated for by the payment of its value, and the loss of a tooth by an appropriate financial retribution as well. Rabbinic literalism thus moves far from the obvious meaning: it is essentially interpretative, and as such not literal in the true sense at all. Even at this first level of reading, the verse already means something different to what it explicitly says or seems to be saying.

The very term "Peshat" is ambiguous and can mean "simple" or "naked". A literal reading is therefore an examination of a naked text, a kind of literary voyeurism. Commentaries and interpretations, on the other hand, weave a membrane around the text's nakedness to clothe its literal sense with new meanings.

Jewish interpretation seems to say that it is impossible – or forbidden – to read a naked text, to leave it uncovered. Insisting on reading it in its nudity is to permit it to express only one truth, one naked truth.

A voyeuristic reading of sacred texts is a threat to readers from all three Abrahamic religions, who often arm themselves with their revealed scriptures to defend a world view which is thus presented as indisputable. Barricaded behind what is seen as an immutable meaning, they often seek to justify the social, political or religious status quo by gagging all other interpretations.

*

The approach taken by literalist readers often suffers from inconsistency. The primary meaning of a text is often discredited without debate, such as judging certain laws as anachronistic, even though they are explicitly promulgated in the Bible. There are few people today lobbying for the stoning of adulterous women, or making enquiries about the correct biblical procedure for purchasing a slave . . . On the other hand, a literal reading is often invoked as a legitimate interpretation of other biblical passages. This is why the Genesis verse "It is not good for man to be alone" (2:18) is taken by some people to be a definitive condemnation of celibacy, or "Do not lie with a male as one lies with a woman" in Leviticus (18:22) appears to make male homosexuality an irremediable abomination.

What is paradoxical about these interpretations is that their defenders rely on a literal reading in some cases but refuse it in others, supporting their claims, as the case may be, with "it is written", or by asserting interpretative distance.

May I lapidate my uncle?

A comic denunciation of the absurdity of fundamentalist readings of the Bible has made the rounds on the internet in the last few years, without its author being identified. An American radio show host, who regularly cited the Bible

(Leviticus) to condemn homosexuality as an abomination, is said to have received the following letter:

Dear Dr. Laura,

Thank you for doing so much to educate people regarding God's Law. I have learned a great deal from your show and try to share that knowledge with as many people as I can. When someone tries to defend the homosexual lifestyle, for example, I simply remind them that Leviticus 18:22 clearly states it to be an abomination . . . End of debate.

I do need some advice from you, however, regarding some other elements of God's Laws and how to follow them.

1. Leviticus 25:44 states that I may possess slaves, both male and female, provided they are purchased from neighbouring nations. A friend of mine claims that this applies to Mexicans, but not Canadians. Can you clarify? Why can't I own Canadians?

2. I would like to sell my daughter into slavery, as sanctioned in Exodus 21:7. In this day and age, what do you think would be a fair price for her?

3. I know that I am allowed no contact with a woman while she is in her period of Menstrual uncleanliness – Lev. 15:19–24. The problem is how do I tell? I have tried asking, but most women take offense.

4. When I burn a bull on the altar as a sacrifice, I know it creates a pleasing odor for the Lord – Lev. 1:9. The problem is my neighbours. They claim the odor is not pleasing to them. Should I smite them?

5. I have a neighbour who insists on working on the Sabbath. Exodus 35:2 clearly states he should be put to death. Am I morally obligated to kill him myself, or should I ask the police to do it?

6. A friend of mine feels that even though eating shellfish is an abomination, Lev. 11:10, it is a lesser abomination than homosexuality. I don't agree. Can you settle this? Are there "degrees" of abomination?

7. Lev. 21:20 states that I may not approach the altar of God if I have a defect in my sight. I have to admit that I wear reading glasses. Does my vision have to be 20/20, or is there some wiggle-room here?

8. Most of my male friends get their hair trimmed, including the hair around their temples, even though this is expressly forbidden by Lev. 19:27. How should they die?

9. I know from Lev. 11:6–8 that touching the skin of a dead pig makes me unclean, but may I still play football if I wear gloves?

10. My uncle has a farm. He violates Lev. 19:19 by planting two different crops in the same field, as does his wife by wearing garments made of two different

kinds of thread (cotton/polyester blend). He also tends to curse and blaspheme a lot. Is it really necessary that we go to all the trouble of getting the whole town together to stone them? Lev. 24:10–16. Couldn't we just burn them to death at a private family affair, like we do with people who sleep with their in-laws? (Lev. 20:14)

I know you have studied these things extensively and thus enjoy considerable expertise in such matters, so I'm confident you can help.

Thank you again for reminding us that God's word is eternal and unchanging.

Your adoring fan,

Anonymous

(It would be a damn shame if we couldn't own a Canadian.)[20]

While this humorous letter forces literalists to face up to their contradictions, it also raises essential theological questions. Which are the Bible verses whose literal meaning we perceive as timeless? Which are those that religious authorities accept as metaphors to be interpreted allegorically, or which qualify as anachronistic?

*

20 See "Dr. Laura and Leviticus", America, August 18, 2020, https://www. americamagazine.org/faith/2010/08/18/dr-laura-and-leviticus.

In principle, a Jewish reading of the Bible consists of clothing the text with commentary, so as not to leave it naked. But one must also recognise that exegesis does not always guarantee a modest reading. Sometimes the clothing fixes a meaning that makes the text even more immodest than if it had been left unclothed. It is important to always cover the scriptures with a veil of human exegesis that is open to change and renewal. This veil, this moving fabric, is what we must now reclaim as a conspicuous sign of interpretative modesty. It is only by covering ourselves with it that we can start the exploration of the texts.

CHAPTER THREE

Adam and the Genesis of Nakedness

Exploring the Bible in search of naked characters reveals quite a few surprises. Many stories include nakedness as a dramatic element with tragic repercussions. As soon as Adam and Eve discover their nakedness, they must leave the Garden of Eden. When Noah disembarks from his ark at the end of the flood, his first acts are to get drunk and disrobe himself, before cursing his grandson. In one of the most famous scenes of jealousy in the Bible, Joseph, the favourite son of the patriarch Jacob, has his tunic torn off him by his brothers, who leave him for dead after throwing him, naked, into a hole.[21]

One could cite numerous other episodes in the Bible where the body is suddenly uncovered, or, on the contrary, where the injunction is firmly made not to reveal another person's nudity under any pretext.[22] What is the exact

---

21 D. Horvilleur, E. Papernik, D. Muskat, "Manteau de protection, manteau de vulnérabilité" (Coat of protection, coat of vulnerability), *Tenou'a*, 147, p. 52.
22 This prohibition is in fact reflected in the architecture of sacred spaces. The high priest is described as approaching the altar of sacrifices on an inclined

meaning of this nakedness that must not be unveiled? What is the meaning of biblical modesty? In order to understand this, we must go back to the genesis of its appearance: the arrival of the first man in history, Adam.

Adam's attire

It's the first time that counts! This is how one might summarise one of the principles of interpretation to which Jewish exegesis particularly adheres. This principle of the first occurrence postulates that the very first appearance of a term or a concept in the Bible is the most critical. A first biblical use of a word is seen as holding its profound meaning, as if everything was already said the first time the word appears.

The first nakedness appears with Adam. In French, as well as English, the expression "in Adam's attire" means in no attire at all. But Adam is not only the first man whose nakedness is described, he is also the first whose nakedness is covered, the first to make himself clothing. Genesis presents him as the first man to be made so uncomfortable by this nakedness that he chooses to cover it. In other words, Adam is the first person in history to display modesty.

*

plane, and not on steps, in order that his "nakedness may not be exposed upon it" (Exodus 20:26).

The story of the creation of man is one of those biblical episodes that are so much part of our culture, our myths and visual or literary representations, that everyone believes that they know it. The first human, modelled out of clay, whom André Chouraqui calls "*le glébeux*" or "the earthy one" – the most exact translation of the Hebrew word *adam*, from "the earth", *adama* – comes to life when the Lord blows the breath of life into his nostrils. Then, after being placed in the Garden of Eden, the man is bored. Because "it is not good for man to be alone" (Genesis 2:18), God takes one of Adam's ribs to make a woman, Eve. This is the story of the birth of the first human couple.

This mythical account has penetrated popular culture so deeply that few people realise that it is not faithful to the biblical text. A careful rereading of the first chapters of the Bible offers a very different version of this foundational episode, and a more subtle and ambiguous one.

The two births of Adam

In the Bible, humankind is born not just once, but twice. More accurately, two apparently contradictory accounts of the appearance of humanity are juxtaposed in Genesis. The first two chapters of the Bible appear to be in opposition to each other, as if reflected in a distorting mirror. In the first account, the Lord creates humankind with two genders. It is said: "God created man in His image [. . .] male and female he created them" (Genesis 1:27). Then, in the second chapter, another version is given: this time God models the man out of soil and places him alone in the Garden of Eden. He then plunges his creature into sleep, and takes away one of his ribs to create the material that he will fashion into a woman. He then presents her to the awakened man, who takes her as his wife.

In one version, humanity is created simultaneously in both genders, male and female, both in the divine image. In the second version, humanity's masculinity constitutes the original model, later amputated of a feminine side. This time, the two sexes of humankind are created in two stages: first the masculine, then the feminine.

How might we reconcile these two versions? How could man and woman be born twice?

Depending on the era, the exegetes have different views on this and don't reconcile the contradictions in the same way. Some modern readers don't reconcile them at all. This is the case in contemporary biblical criticism, as it developed in the Jewish and Christian world in the nineteenth century, which sees these two contradictory accounts as proof of two different versions having been subsequently adjoined. These accounts are considered to be from different authors and editors, and to have both been integrated at a later date into the biblical canon. This theory of the delayed compilation of two (or more) sources spares the reader any attempt at reconciliation of the two versions.

Of course, this thesis cannot satisfy traditional commentators, for whom the revealed origin of the sacred texts forbids the possibility of a composite anthology of dissonant accounts. From their point of view, it is imperative to consider the text as consistent. This is what the Jewish tradition proposes, through various commentaries that give the text back its unity, despite the contradictions. Indeed there are several Jewish legends that provide a reconciliation of the contradictory narratives of the first two chapters of Genesis.

The rebellious or maternal female

One of these legends presents a primal female character, a sort of proto-Eve, who is mentioned in rabbinical literature. Numerous texts from the beginning of the Common Era and the Middle Ages refer to a woman said to be the one from the first chapter of the Bible, the one created at the same time as the first man, which explains the verse "male and female they were created". Chapter 1 of Genesis thus narrates the creation of Adam and an ante-Eve.

In order to affirm that such a primal creature could have

existed, even when the Bible text does not refer to her by name, the first Jewish commentators point to the verse in Chapter 2 of Genesis, where it is written that when Eve was created, Adam declared on seeing her: "This one at last Is bone of my bones And flesh of my flesh. This one shall be called Woman, For from man was she taken" (Genesis 2:23). The words "at last", which might initially appear to be superfluous, are in fact the single piece of evidence supporting the claim by exegetists who see it as proof that there was a first time, in other words that there was formerly another woman placed by Adam's side. She is said to have disappeared from history and the text because she was incapable of satisfying him. In rabbinical literature, this woman's name is Lilith, a mysterious character, who is mentioned in Mesopotamian and Canaanite mythology and associated in these cultures with a demonic and malevolent power, threatening men and their homes.

Why does she have this reputation? How are we to understand this original repudiation? A rabbinical legend from the first centuries recounts the surprising episode that led to Lilith being expelled from Genesis, to her not staying at Adam's side either in Eden or in the text. These accounts make her out to be a demanding "feminist" before her time. Her divorce from Adam and her exile from Genesis are said to be due to a strange dispute between the original couple: "Lilith left Adam because she did not want to lie under him during conjugal relations: she felt she was his equal."[23] It is thus because of Lilith's demand for equality and her rejection of submission, symbolised in the text as sexual submission, that God appears to have allowed Lilith to emancipate herself from the account, and to have created a second, more docile woman. Hence the presence of these two apparently contradictory chapters in Genesis. The first woman was born from a simultaneous creation of humankind as both male and female; this is something that might have made her, according to the rabbis, too insolent and demanding. The birth of the other woman from the rib of the man, coming second to a primary male body, would make her a humbler and more submissive being. It is she who becomes the mother of humanity, whereas Lilith is condemned to roam the world, tempting men by turning them away from the path of virtue. The two women of Genesis are thus contrasting figures of motherhood and female temptation.

The thesis of androgyny

To reconcile the first two chapters of Genesis without having recourse to a demonic female, Jewish literature also proposes a so-called "androgynous" reading of the creation

23 From the collection of rabbinical legends Bereishit Rabbah, compiled in the fifth century. Quoted in Otzar Midrashim, ed. J. D. Eisenstein (New York: J. D. Eisenstein, 1915).

of man. According to this thesis, developed notably in the central book of Jewish mysticism, the Zohar, the first Adam was a model of androgynous humankind, bearing two genders. This is the literal reading of the verse "male and female he created them". A man with two faces and two genders was created in a single body.

According to this reading, the second chapter of Genesis would describe a later separation, what Jewish tradition calls the original severance. Using the first anaesthetic in history, the great divine "surgeon" plunged man into sleep and separated the two genders with his scalpel, the two sides of an androgynous being, to create a humankind with two distinct sexes. One can easily see how this account and this reading might reconcile the contradictions in the text. From the being with two genders of the first chapter spring the two differentiated and sexual beings of the remainder of the text.

This traditional reading presents several similarities with the Platonic myth of the origin of the sexes. In Plato's *Symposium*, humankind is described by Aristophanes as being androgynous. Zeus then separated this androgynous being into two halves to limit its power, thus forming a humankind with two genders. According to Plato, this original separation is in fact what explains the phenomenon of love, as a sense of nostalgia for a lost unity and a desperate quest for one's other half.

Much closer to our time, Sigmund Freud writes in 1929, in a note to *Civilization and its Discontents*, that "man is an animal organism with (like others) an unmistakably bisexual disposition. The individual corresponds to a fusion of two symmetrical halves, of which, according to some investigators, one is purely male and the other female. It is equally possible that each half was originally hermaphrodite. [. . .] The theory of bi-sexuality is still surrounded by many obscurities."[24]

In this reading, two genders arise from an androgynous genesis of humankind, differentiated in their tasks and destinies, and fated to live side by side.

The side, or rib, raises another question which deserves its own exegesis: why does the severance occur only on a lateral bone? Why is the separated female, the Eve to be, born precisely from that part of the anatomy? What if this was all just a misunderstanding, with gigantic repercussions? What if it was just due to an error in translation?

24 Sigmund Freud, "Civilization and its Discontents", in *The Standard Edition of the Complete Psychological Works of Sigmund Freud, Vol. XXI*, ed. James Strachey (London: Vintage, 2001), p. 105.

The Hebrew word used in Genesis and translated as "rib" in most editions of the Bible is *tzela*. This word, when used elsewhere in the Bible, is always translated as "side" and not "rib".[25]

God plunged the first Adam into sleep to separate the feminine side – and not the rib – from the masculine side. The difference in translation may seem trivial, but it carries heavy consequences. In one case, the "rib" woman is a constructed object, a bone, in other words a partial structure sculpted from a complete man. She is a bit of him, a supporting element that takes on a life of its own but remains dependent, because of its origin, on the first, masculine body. In the other case, the "side" woman is the division of an original androgynous being henceforth cut into two. She is another subject, and not an object, just as the man is. In this version, both genders are cut off, separated from the primary undivided entity that they had constituted.

Over the centuries, the theorisation of the relationship between men and women in our culture has largely been built and maintained on the basis of the first of these translations and not the second: on a model of woman as a rib of Adam's, not a side of Adam's, and perceived as a partial object derived from an almost complete and virile

25 See for example Exodus 26:20, where the word *tzela* defines the side, not the rib, of the tabernacle.

body. Perhaps all it took was one (poor) translation for this to happen.

There are numerous incorrect translations in the Bible that have had considerable political or cultural implications. Indeed, Adam's rib is far from the only example of an erroneous or partial translation of Genesis. Another famous example of a translation with remarkable consequences is that of the forbidden fruit in the original Paradise.

The apple given by Eve to Adam has figured in representations of this mythical scene throughout history, from Renaissance paintings to contemporary advertising banners. However, this fruit does not appear anywhere in the Hebrew text of Genesis. There is of course a tree, standing in the middle of the garden and whose fruit it is forbidden to eat, but neither the species nor the fruit of the tree are mentioned.

No doubt it is the Latin translation that is to blame for this misunderstanding. The tree in the Garden of Eden is defined as the "tree of the knowledge of good and bad" (Genesis 2:9); in the Latin translation known as the Vulgate, we read "*lignum scientiae boni et mali*". Because Christendom had for centuries read the Bible exclusively in Latin, the "bad" (*malus*, here the genitive *mali*) came to be read as its homonym, "*malus*", the apple. Wordplay, or a mistaken reading?

The rabbinical tradition never mentions an apple, but raises the hypothesis of other fruits that could be borne by the tree of knowledge. The Talmud suggests that it could be a fig tree or a grapevine. Why these fruits? After tasting the fruit, the man and woman cover their nakedness with a fig leaf, which leads commentators to think that this tree was not far away, perhaps even close at hand.

Adam and Eve suddenly realise they are naked. Their perception is altered. What if the fruit was from a grapevine, from which wine is made? The first inebriation in history might be the origin of the knowledge of good and evil.

Apple, fig, grape – does it matter? Not at all, except for interpretative closure. Once the apple was "canonised" by Christendom, the tree no longer appears in the popular imagination in any other form. The forbidden fruit is defined and specified, once and for all, by a translation that allows for no ambiguity. The fruit henceforth has an image, a smell, a taste, and discourages any other possible readings. The interpretation is thus fixed.

Marc-Alain Ouaknin defines this as the "apple complex": an "attitude to the world and to knowledge that leads to the spreading of rumours, of prejudices, of hearsay, of fake images and ideas, which are never properly questioned and become popular knowledge with the standing of truth."[26]

This definition can be applied to any interpretation that closes off other reading possibilities. All translations are

26 Marc-Alain Ouaknin, *Zeugma: Mémoire biblique et déluges contemporains* (Zeugma: biblical memory and contemporary deluges) (Paris: Le Seuil, 2008), p. 505.

treason, but some of them condemn the text to the detention of a single meaning.

Knowing one's nakedness or knowing one's wife

Adam is the first man whose nakedness is described. Like many biblical terms, the notion of nudity is more ambiguous than it may seem, and it is worth exploring its etymology. In polysemic Hebrew, it is not uncommon for a single word or root to mean two very different things, or even to mean both one thing and its opposite, depending on the context.

"To be naked" in Hebrew is *arum*. But this term has multiple meanings in the Bible. In the first paragraphs of Genesis, naked Adam is said to be *arum*. But *arum* is also used of the serpent, the other key character in the narrative, described as "cunning". One single word in Hebrew means both naked and cunning, two notions that seem to be contradictory: the transparency of clothing and the opacity of intentions, the uncovered body and hidden plans.

Clothing also carries semantic ambiguity in Hebrew. The word *beged*, which means "garment", also means "treason". Clothing is what hides the truth, it is a lie worn on the body. This idea of the lying garment is found elsewhere in Hebrew: a coat (*me'il*) also means "fraud", and sometimes even marital infidelity.

In Numbers (5:12), the Bible warns against a woman who "makes her husband wear a coat"[27] or, in other words, who commits adultery. The coat of the biblical cuckold replaces the horns of other cultures. It evokes what is outwardly obvious, cannot escape the gaze of others, what can be publicly mocked or ridiculed, in short, what is worn by someone who has had "the wool pulled over his eyes". If, in Hebrew, nakedness is a synonym for cunning and clothing a synonym for falsehood, what, then, is the attire of truth?

Taste and knowledge

"She took of its fruit and ate. She also gave some to her husband, and he ate. Then the eyes of both of them were opened and they perceived that they were naked."
[Genesis 3:6–7]

In Genesis the ingestion of the forbidden fruit alters the consciousness of man and gives him a new and different insight into the world. He has to taste it to know. Transgression gives access to a previously impossible or forbidden vision: the awareness of nakedness. It is difficult to imagine that man had not, until then, known that he was naked. Of what blinding naivety was he the victim?

27 Author's translation.

The Christian interpretation often associates original innocence with a pre-sexual era. The exile of humanity from its innocent childhood is seen as determined by its access to guilty sexuality. This is not the traditional Jewish reading, which does not perceive the error in Genesis to be sexual. Judaism does not link chastity and innocence. In its world view, human sexuality pre-existed the consumption of the fruit. The man knows the woman before knowing his own nakedness. Before the episode of the tree, we read that the man "clings to his wife, so that they become one flesh" (Genesis 2:24). This physical union precedes any transgression and is not guilty in any way.

The Talmud and rabbinical literature develop a largely positive rhetoric of sexuality and desire. In numerous texts, the sexual drive is not only tolerated but described as necessary. Desire is sometimes qualified as an "evil inclination" (*yetzer hara* in Hebrew) but this inclination is what provides the necessary impetus for the renewal of life and permits the world to exist. Sexual desire is, in some sense, the "libido" of the world and appears in numerous Jewish sources as the condition of the maintenance of our universe. "But without the Evil Desire, however, no man would build a house, take a wife and beget children" (Genesis Rabbah 9:7[28]). Creation and human engagement with the world depend on

28 Author's translation.

the sexual urge. It is therefore not from virginal innocence but from another state that man extricates himself by eating the forbidden fruit.

From that point on, man knows that he is naked and can therefore no longer stay naked. Just before expelling Adam and Eve from the Garden of Eden, God fashions a strange parting gift, "garments of skins for Adam and his wife" (Genesis 3:21). There's no question of them leaving without getting dressed.

A short treatise on biblical dermatology

What is this divinely sewn garment of skins with which God clothes man? Is it just to keep him warm, or to protect him from the dangers that might assail him outside the shelter of the Garden of Eden?

Jewish commentators have torn each other to shreds regarding the nature of this item of clothing. According to some, the serpent was the animal sacrificed to make this coat (Midrash Tehillim 42, Pirkei DeRabbi Eliezer 20:3). It was the snake, the bearer of temptation, the great culprit of the preceding episode, who paid for it with his skin . . . unless of course it just sloughed off in his regular moult. In other commentaries (notably in the Zohar, but also in the accounts by Philo of Alexandria) a more surprising idea can be found: the material from which God sews the tunic is none other than man's own skin. This reading has the audacity to suggest that in the Garden of Eden humanity was a-dermal, had no skin at all: not that it had been skinned alive, but that it was just naturally without a dermal membrane . . . Nakedness in the Garden of Eden is thus considered a dermatological issue. The exile from Paradise forces us to cover ourselves with a layer that we did not originally possess. In the original world of the Garden of Eden, man lacks the membrane that separates him from the world. From then onwards, he is endowed with a corporeal boundary, a limit placed between him and what surrounds him.

Whereas in Paradise man was transparent to his neighbour, he is henceforth made opaque by a covering of skin. The Fall is therefore considered not to be the loss of innocence, but to be the end of a luminous and translucent state which is followed by the entrance into an obscured world. We pass from a world of transparency to a world of covering.

In Eden, man is not aware of his nakedness because he is not aware of a separation between himself and the world. Henceforth, the infinite transparency shrivels up like Balzac's wild ass's skin. The man perceives the membranes of the world, and therefore also his own. He knows that he is naked, and that others may gaze upon him. This is how the need to cover oneself is born. When one is transparent, there is no need to hide oneself. When one ceases to be transparent, one then feels too naked to be uncovered.

This is the first instance of human modesty, according to the Bible: in the beginning everything is one, including humanity, and described as "male and female". From one andro-gynous, unseparated body, man and woman, cut from each other, will henceforth be two. And the bodies of these two beings will be separated by a membrane.

The departure from Eden marks the entry into a world where porosity between beings is limited, or at the very least, where humans no longer perceive a total permeability to each other. In this world, nakedness and modesty have meaning. One knows one is naked only when one is partially covered, when one is already a membranous being, a being on whose surface there are sensors that allow us to perceive what is exterior to us.

Ashamed but not guilty

Adam and Eve ate the fruit that was forbidden to them. Questioned about their responsibility, they answer: it wasn't me, it was someone else! "It wasn't me, it was the woman," says Adam, "The woman You put at my side – she gave me of the tree and I ate" (Genesis 3:12). Then it is the woman's turn to say: "The serpent duped me, and I ate" (Genesis 3:13).

The art of laying the blame elsewhere is equally shared from creation onwards: neither sex escapes it.

It is perhaps because of this foundational account of what Christianity calls "original sin" that some people consider the feeling of guilt to be what lies at the heart of so-called "Judeo-Christian morality". But this classic accusation is not one that can be easily proved: is guilt really the issue in the account of the original transgression?

Before their transgression, Adam and Eve are described thus: "The two of them were naked, the man and his wife, yet they felt no shame" (Genesis 2:25). Just after their transgression, they are found hiding in a tree to try to avoid the eyes of God. Shame appears, but there is no mention of their feeling guilty.

What difference is there between shame and guilt? It would be a mistake to confuse these two feelings, which deserve to be clearly differentiated. According to Boris Cyrulnik, "guilt belongs to the universe of the mistake. We feel guilty, we must make up for it, expiate, mend it. Shame has nothing to do with it. Shame places an intimate detractor inside us that eats away at us, destroys us, devalues us. Whoever feels shame does not want to make amends, they distance themselves from others, wish that the ground would swallow them up, try to escape from the sight of others".[29]

29 *Le Point*, September 2, 2010.

Guilt can exist independently of the presence of others. We can feel guilty alone or in company, with or without being seen by another person. Shame, however, necessarily involves an external gaze, or the imaginary sense of that gaze. We feel ashamed to know or imagine that someone has witnessed or found out about our actions.

According to Serge Tisseron, shame "creates a rupture in the continuity of the subject. The image they have of themselves is distorted, they lose their bearings, both spatial and temporal, they have no memory and no future."[30] Tisseron posits that shame is, first, a feeling of being cut off from oneself, or from the group whose gaze threatens to decompose you. That feeling is thus an internal rupture, in other words a disconnect between the idealised image one has of oneself and the image perceived through the gaze of another person. The feeling of shame is eminently incarnated and visceral. It generally provokes a loss of bodily control: the ground vanishes beneath our feet, we wish we could disappear. The most frequent manifestation of shame is blushing, a form of loss of control of our epidermis, the sensation of the face being suddenly flayed, heated and visible. To blush is to "know one is naked".

*

30 *La Honte: Psychanalyse d'un lien social* (Shame: psychoanalysis of a social bond) (Paris: Dunod "Psychismes", 1992).

In Hebrew, shame is *bushah*, a term whose root has another meaning in biblical writing: it is often used to describe a situation of separation, a delayed encounter with another person who is late in arriving.[31] Etymologically, the word refers to the idea of an unsatisfied expectation, an impossible reunion with another person's body. Hebrew therefore has only one root, which means shame and lack. In Hebraic thinking, this feeling is inextricably linked with the idea of cutting, the awareness of a separation, a "rupture in the continuity of the subject".

That is precisely the feeling born in the Garden of Eden: shame is the fruit of humanity's new awareness. It arises when humans have a skin that separates them from others, others who can look at them, and from whom they can be separated. In the beginning, in a body with no membrane or boundary, lack does not exist. No separation is perceived or felt. Nothing and nobody is lacking because nothing and nobody is out of sight, or outside of oneself. In such a universe, shame does not exist and neither does modesty.

Then the man and the woman are suddenly "dermal". Henceforth and for ever, they will be two. Perceiving

31 Two examples of the occurrence of this root: in Exodus (32:1), Moses climbs Mount Sinai. Seeing that he was "so long in coming down", the people become impatient and lose courage. In Judges (5:28), Sisera's mother is desperately waiting for the return home of her son and is worried that his chariot is so long in coming.

themselves as each cut off from the other, they are truly naked. It is from this nakedness that shame is born, as the awareness of rupture and lack.

But equally, this shame is what creates the very possibility of an encounter. In Hebrew, "to seal an alliance" is said "to cut an alliance": we can only approach someone if we have been separated. It is precisely through cutting that the path towards another person is opened up. The other person is the one whose gaze we seek, but to whom we do not wish to show ourselves completely naked.

The modesty of a garment is therefore not what definitively pushes back the gaze, but what creates a delay, a latency in vision and connection. The exit from Paradise is not an original transgression, but a necessary division that arises from fusion and is the precondition of any encounter. Shame, as it appears at the genesis of humanity, is not only without guilt, but is in fact precisely what opens us to others. It is "the (never complete) unveiling of lovers one to the other (but therefore also their secret) [which] guarantees the space of alterity necessary for the kind of desire that is not the appropriation of the other's body".[32] It is because Adam and Eve are separated that they are now ready to meet each other. The skin that separates them makes them seek

32 Michel Sanchez-Cardenas, "*La pudeur, un lieu de liberté?* de Monique Selz" (Modesty, a space of freedom? by Monique Selz), in *Revue française de psychanalyse*, 68 (2004), pp. 699–702.

one another out. The first biblical model of modesty is the recognition of an otherness that escapes us, with which we can never be one, and whose boundaries we must respect.

The origin of the world

Our journey through the scriptures necessarily had to start in the Garden of Eden, alongside a still naked humanity which could not remain so much longer. Outside Eden, Adam and Eve are (at last) opaque to one another. It is because they have something to hide, a skin to cover them, that they set out in search of each other. This is our condition, as "dermic" beings: it is because we are conscious (and often ashamed) of our limitations that we are careful not to display everything, that we cover our failings. It is also thanks to these failings and this lack that we are able to seek company outside ourselves.

This takes us a long way from what fundamentalist religious discourse so often proffers: the injunction to veil a guilty body, to cut ourselves off from a threatening alterity. The genesis of real modesty is a culture of encounter, not of distancing. As such, veiling anyone to stifle desire rather than to arouse it is not only nonsensical but culpable.

CHAPTER FOUR

Noah: Rising Naked from the Waters

The exploration of modesty in the Bible leads us directly to another famous episode from Genesis. This one comes shortly after the departure from Eden, and tells of the nakedness of another hero, the man of the flood.

We are ten generations away from Adam and Eve. Humanity has left Paradise, dressed in a divinely fashioned garment of skin. But quite soon the supreme tailor, like an haute couture designer, is no longer so sure about his models. He starts to doubt his creations and is disappointed by humanity. Genesis then states: "And the Lord regretted that He had made man on earth, and his heart was saddened" (Genesis 6:6).

Disappointed, dissatisfied, he is ready to erase everything since the beginning of the book. The flood comes to sweep it all away. In the space of a few chapters, humanity is born and dies. The Bible recounts the creation and de-creation in turn. It juxtaposes in stark proximity a process of edification and an account of its deconstruction. The waters, separated in the beginning, come together once more. The dry land, which had barely just appeared, is engulfed. The destructive flood occurs as a systematic reversal of the creation which has just been described.

In the original account, nothing survives, except a unique sampling of previous life: one single family, Noah's, and one single pair of each of the animals that he has taken care to place in a floating ark. The animals enter this mythical embarkation two by two, in matching pairs. It will be their task to repopulate the earth, after the Creator is appeased.

Like his ancestor, Noah is a founding father. According to the story in the Bible, he and his wife are the sole ancestors of the entire postdiluvian population. Their three children are called Shem, Japheth and Ham, meaning "name", "beautiful", and "hot", respectively. In another translation, they are the person you hear, the person you see, and the person you touch. This is how the primordial biblical genealogy is written, where these names and their translations whisper the poetry of an ancient world and the essence of those that bear them.

A world is reborn from this fraternal trio. According to the traditional exegesis, each of the brothers becomes, in archetypal fashion, the ancestor of a continent or a geographical zone. Shem is seen as the ancestor of the Semites, who bear his name. Japheth is said to be the father of Europe and of Western civilisations. And Ham is said to have populated Africa with his descendants. This myth of postdiluvian origins sets all of humanity in a fraternal bond, telling the story of how all humans came out as brothers from a shipwrecked ark, surviving a lost world together. But the unity of this second draft of humanity will soon be dissolved.

Noah rising from the waters

Noah is the ancestor of the humans who have populated the earth, bearing on his shoulders the future of humankind. But he is also an antihero, whose nakedness and weakness the Bible soon reveals in an unsettling account. This episode, less well known than the story of the ark, has nevertheless been the subject of copious exegesis.

As his family and the animals disembark onto dry land, the hero and his sons' new life is related in this way:

> The sons of Noah who came out of the Ark were Shem, Ham, and Japheth – Ham being the father of Canaan. These three were the sons of Noah, and from these the whole world branched out. Noah, the tiller of the soil, was the first to plant a vineyard. He drank of the wine and became drunk, and he uncovered himself within his tent. Ham, the father of Canaan, saw his father's nakedness and told his two brothers outside. But Shem and Japheth took a cloth, placed it

against both their backs and, walking backward, they covered their father's nakedness; their faces were turned the other way, so that they did not see their father's nakedness. When Noah woke up from his wine and learned what his youngest son had done to him, he said, "Cursed be Canaan; the lowest of slaves shall he be to his brothers. [Genesis 9:18–25]

Noah at last sets foot on dry land and is soon pitching and rolling with drink. The patriarch, having survived the flood, plants a vineyard from which he harvests the wine, then he drinks to excess, and once inebriated, denudes himself.

Any attentive reader of this passage will see that there are numerous inconsistencies here, and several mysterious series of events that raise certain questions: why is the man who voyaged for weeks at sea on board his ark suddenly called "the tiller of the soil"? Why is this man's first act on dry land to plant a vineyard? Does he get drunk deliberately? Why does he denude himself in his tent after getting drunk? Why does Ham, his son, look at what his brothers refuse to see? Why, when he awakes, does Noah punish the grandson for the acts of his father?

None of these questions have escaped the commentators, who have undertaken a centuries-long exegesis, akin to a surgical examination, or a painstaking archaeological exploration of the strata in the text.

Out of the (drunken) boat

At the end of the flood, something goes wrong for the founding family of humanity. After forty days of isolation on the open sea, the bond between the generations is troubled by discord. It's when they reach dry land that everything capsizes.

Noah knows that he is called upon to reconstruct humankind in the giant graveyard of the postdiluvian world. This man, whose entire generation has disappeared, voyaged for forty days over death, and must now build life on the bones of his generation.

His first initiative is to plant, to give roots to future growth. But he gets drunk from that plant. The product of life that is reborn on earth is also what makes Noah once again leave solid ground, cast off and float away into drunkenness. Noah anchors himself by planting, and immediately tears himself away from the new reality by consuming the fruit.

Consuming the fruit as a transgression: this is of course a biblical déjà vu for the reader. The descendant of Adam plays out the scene of his origins. We are projected once again into the Garden of Eden. A tree is in the middle of the garden. The ingestion of its fruit again modifies human consciousness. According to the rabbis, this tree of the new world might well bear the same forbidden fruit as the one in the Garden of Eden (remember, it is not an apple). For the commentators, it is the same tree and therefore the same action. The transgression is repeated, history is stuttering.

The Talmud affirms that Noah should "have learned from Adam, the first man, whose banishment from the Garden of Eden was caused only by wine" (Babylon Talmud, Sanhedrin 70a). But he was not able to learn the lesson of his forebear's experience. Unless he believed himself to be stronger than his ancestor, capable of surmounting anything after the trial of the flood.

Noah is the heir of Adam. Perhaps this is why he is called "*ish ha'adama*" – not a "man of the earth (*adama*)" as the translation so often suggests, but a "man of the lineage of Adam". And yet his consumption of the fruit has the opposite result of his ancestor's only a few generations earlier. Adam discovered himself to be naked and covered himself, but Noah, when drunk, undresses and lies down naked in the middle of his tent.

Noah has just spent forty days in his ark, a giant womb that protects the gestation of new life on earth. According to rabbinical law, forty days is the time it takes for an embryo to form in its mother's body and to develop the organs of a foetus (Babylon Talmud, Yevamot treatise 69b). Noah has just been delivered by his mother-vessel and thrown onto dry land. The anchor is barely dropped before he regresses. One can imagine him lying naked, in a foetal position, like a newborn baby in its crib.

*

Noah, the new first man, is a man in regression. His nakedness represents an attempt to return to the original state, to the Garden of Eden, to the time before clothing. Intoxicated by the illusion of a return to Paradise, Noah, in his drunkenness, returns to the unified world from before the rupture. In his womb-tent, he takes refuge in a world before exile, before death, trauma and loss. But another trauma, another transgression is about to wrench him out again and exile him from his alcoholic garden.

Ham's fault?

What actually happened in Noah's tent? Which action is his son's real transgression? Let us return to the two elliptical lines that describe his mistake: "Ham, the father of Canaan, saw his father's nakedness and told his two brothers outside" (Genesis 9:22).

Was Ham not supposed to see anything, or not supposed to say anything? Is his transgression connected to the sight of a forbidden body or to his account of that sight? Is it the violation of private space that is culpable, or is it the lack of discretion, which should have been the mark of filial respect? For traditional commentators, it is not really about either of these. Ham's transgression is not a question of sight or word, but of action. Their conviction is based on the verse that immediately follows the account, where it is said that Noah wakes up, regains consciousness after his intoxication, and then learns "what his youngest son had done to him" (Genesis 9:24).

Would a furtive look or a hasty word leave such a mark as to give rise to that intimate conviction? What act might have left a trace so perceptible on awakening, and especially so likely to arouse the father's anger? Noah's son must have "done" something far beyond sight and word. The Talmud states it unequivocally: Ham violated or castrated his father (Babylon Talmud, Sanhedrin 70a).

Even if this act is not made explicit in the verse itself, according to tradition the transgression is incontestably of a sexual nature. The father's "nakedness is seen", a biblical expression which commentators always interpret as describing sexual relations. The sight of a naked body implicitly catalyses or announces the sexual act.

This over-reading might be considered somewhat fanciful, even excessively so. We might prefer to limit ourselves to a closer, literal reading of the text which is less sexual. But by pushing back against the limits of explicit meaning, the tradition invites us to explore the true essence of Ham's transgression and the way it is inscribed in the transgenerational story.

In Noah's life, spaces repeatedly appear to be violated: a family lives in isolation, in the extreme intimacy of a boat, with no way out during the forty days of its voyage. Once land has been regained, Noah at last establishes a private space in his tent. But the boundary of this refuge is immediately forced. His world is penetrated through his tent, and perhaps even his own body. We can see how there has been a violation of the boundary of a private space, an act of violence committed against the father in his body or his property, whose borders have become permeable and therefore vulnerable to intrusion.

In his book *Messengers of God*,[33] Elie Wiesel considers Noah to be the incarnation of the survivor of a catastrophe. He represents the figure of the traumatised man, who is then the victim of yet another trauma, this time experienced in his own tent, whose repercussions will be felt far beyond his generation. According to rabbinical readings, Noah is violated or castrated, wounded in his flesh, his skin torn off.

Skinless

The word "trauma" was originally used to mean a skin lesion (it is the Greek word for a "wound"). Sigmund Freud uses this idea of a torn-off dermal surface to construct the psychoanalytical concept that plays such a determining role

33 *Messengers of God: Biblical Portraits and Legends*, tr. Marion Wiesel (New York: Random House, 1976).

in his theories, calling trauma a "foreign body which, long after its irruption, continues to play an active role".[34] The body and the mind are invaded by it.

Noah's nakedness speaks of nothing else. A son penetrates his father's space. But where does the space of the father end and the space of the son begin? In this biblical family that floated for so long on the water, is there a leakage problem between the family members?

In her book *Escape from Selfhood*, Ilany Kogan discusses her psychoanalytical work with generations of survivors of catastrophes and genocides.[35] She examines the difficulties some of them have in setting boundaries or separating between the generations. Those traumatised sometimes find it hard to keep their children "out of their tent", to exclude them from their intimate, hyper-private sphere. And so the damage often crosses the intergenerational membrane. Trauma creates an excessive permeability between people.

As discussed in the previous chapter, the expulsion from the Garden of Eden marks the end of a unified world and the entry into a time when we can no longer be at one with each other. Adam "knows he is naked" because henceforth man is irremediably separated from his neighbour by

34   See Sigmund Freud and Joseph Breuer, *Studies in Hysteria*, tr. Nicola Luckhurst (London: Penguin, 2004).
35   Ilany Kogan, *Escape from Selfhood: Breaking Boundaries and Craving for Oneness* (London: Routledge, 2007).

membranes that cover him like a skin. It is this surface which man modestly covers, in order to be able to slowly uncover it and approach the Other.

The episode with Noah, the second nude of the Bible story, is a reworked version of the preceding one. Noah tries to regress, to return to the lost Paradise. Where his ancestor gains in awareness, Noah loses some, so that in his intoxication he no longer realises he is naked. He plays the scene of his origins backwards: Adam and Eve emerge from an original state of fusion, realise they are naked and cover themselves, whereas Noah uncovers himself in order to try to return to that original state. But the story cannot be written in reverse, nor innocence regained, and biblical justice is harsh: when the temptation to return to a state of fusion takes over, the skin is torn off. This leads to trauma.

In this second account from Genesis, modesty is again the implicit recognition of the separateness of others. This separation is not culpable, but necessary. Attempting to completely unveil others is to violate them.

Modesty is what is supposed to protect the relationship from being approached too brutally. Within a couple or a family, where the temptation to "be as one" is the strongest, modesty is the distance that guarantees connection, between individuals and between generations.

This is perhaps how Canaan, the grandson of Noah, becomes the victim of the story in spite of himself. Canaan, the grandson who is punished by his grandfather for his father's transgression, is cursed at the end of the episode, even though he is absent from the scene of the transgression of which neither he nor his descendants are the agents. In a supreme injustice, he will have to pay for something that preceded him and in which he was not involved. The punishment skips a generation and breaks the causal link between acts and their repercussions. He who humiliated his father sees his son humiliated in turn, as "Canaan becomes a slave for his brothers".

But what is a slave if not someone whose space and rights are violated by another who calls himself his master? The slave is precisely the one whose boundaries are transgressed, because he has none of his own. He is dependent on another, deprived of freedom and autonomy.

It appears that the one who has been traumatised here, whose skin is pierced or torn off, runs the risk, in turn, of breaking the membranes of others and transgressing a boundary.

This is, in a way, what Noah affirms when he says: "Cursed be Canaan;/ The lowest of slaves/ Shall he be to his brothers" (Genesis 9:25). This is the warning of a father to his children: the son who violates his father's space runs the risk of seeing his own son's territory violated in turn.

How symbolic it is, then, that the name of the cursed child at the start of Genesis is Canaan. The land of Canaan, in the rest of the book, is in fact one of the names for the Hebrews' Promised Land, the one that will become the land of Israel. That land is where, even today, boundaries appear so difficult to set, and limits are constantly pierced, modified, contested. It is a land where the trauma of the fathers falls so violently on their sons.

The blessing of covering

The Hebrews do not see themselves as the heirs of Ham or Canaan, but as the heirs of Shem, the ancestor of the Semites, as their name indicates. This claimed heritage is not so much an issue of ethnicity or geography as of traditions and morals. In the mysterious account of the profaned tent, Shem is the one who wishes to protect his father's nakedness at all cost:

> Shem and Japheth took a cloth, placed it against both their backs and, walking backward, they covered their father's nakedness; their faces were turned the other way, so that they did not see their father's nakedness. [Genesis 9:23]

Shem thereafter becomes the incarnation of modesty, or the refusal of a forbidden or transgressive sight, which is held up as a value in rabbinical literature. He is the one who covers not only his father but also his own eyes, and convinces his brother Japheth to do the same. In the account, respect is shown through non-vision, through draping the body and recovering dignity.

Being the heir of Shem is to take one's place in the lineage bearing his name (which, let us remember, is the Hebrew word for "name"). It means to prioritise hearing over sight. Shem refuses to see, and carries the cover on his shoulders. For biblical commentators, this act will accord him a very particular blessing.

An Andalusian rabbi and philosopher of the eleventh century, Rabbeinu Bahya, declares that Shem, from that episode onwards, is the bearer of "the mitzvah (command-ment) – to cover oneself". He is referring here to a specific Jewish ritual which, in his eyes, is a heritage from this ancestral story: the wearing of the tallith. The tallith is a prayer shawl, traditionally worn by men in the synagogue. It is a stole with fringes in which men (and women, in the liberal Jewish world) envelop themselves. They first wind it around their face, hiding their eyes, then spread the fabric over their shoulders. Covering themselves so that they can-not see, every time they pray, is the Jews' way of returning into Noah's tent.

The Tallith with eyes closed

In *Veils*, Jacques Derrida speaks at some length about his attachment to his prayer shawl. He writes: "My reference cloth was neither a veil nor a canvas [*une toile*], but a shawl. A prayer shawl I like to touch more than to see, to caress every day, to kiss even without opening my eyes or even when it remains wrapped in a paper bag into which I stick my hand at night, eyes closed [. . .] *Voilà* another skin, but one incomparable to any other skin, to any possible article of clothing [. . .] it is worn in memory of the Law."[36]

Touch or speech are more important for Derrida than sight. In his relationship to his shawl, the issue of the skin arises again, that skin grafted onto a-dermic Adam on his exit from Paradise, that second skin placed by a son on Noah, who was flayed and traumatised in his body and soul. Shem's clothing is an inherited skin we slip over our own in prayer.

But in order to conform to Jewish law, the "skin" of the tallith must possess a characteristic feature: fringes on all four sides (Numbers 15:38–40). The fringes are sometimes visible, coming out of the pockets or the clothing of those who wear them, like the unravelled threads of a badly mended jacket. These fringes have a name in Hebrew, with a strange

36   Hélène Cixous and Jacques Derrida, *Veils*, tr. Geoffrey Bennington (Stanford, CA: Stanford University Press, 2001), pp. 42–3.

sound: *tzitzit*. This word comes from a root that means "to look through" or "to observe through a crack". The tzitzit is a thread that seems to say, almost like an onomatopoeia: "Tsss . . . Tsss . . . look over there!"[37]

These fringes are literally an invitation to look "through", creating a kind of filter that inspires desire. The paradox is interesting and poetic: the prayer garment, the one that reminds us of the necessity of turning our gaze away from others' nakedness, is also a prism for looking between the lines, for the desire to see through transparency.

This is one of the meanings of the tallith (its sense or its decency): a veil, or a skin, which refuses direct sight but invites mediated sight. The vision of the Other through the cracks, "where the garment gapes", as in Roland Barthes' definition of eroticism,[38] arises through an averted gaze, neither direct nor violent, but as sharp as a suggestion.

It is this sensuality that Derrida describes when he says that "the secret of the shawl envelops one single body [. . .] from which it seems to emanate, like an intimate secretion".[39]

As a manifestation of modesty, the shawl or covering

37 The root is found, notably, in the Song of Songs (2:9): when the erotic tension between a shepherd and a shepherdess is at its peak, this term is used to say that the "beloved observes through the trellis" the woman he loves.
38 *The Pleasure of the Text*, tr. Richard Millar (New York: Farrar, Straus and Giroux, 1975), p. 9.
39 *Veils*, p. 44.

is an emanation of the body. It is what filters sight in order not to reveal everything. What it keeps secret allows the intimate relationship not to be violated.

The shawl and the courtesan

There is a colourful story in a Talmudic text where the tallith plays a peculiar role: a wise man heard about a magnificent courtesan who lived in a far-off country. He could not help but make an appointment to meet her, and to cross the oceans to find her. But when he undressed before her, as he took off his clothes, the fringes of his Tallith slapped him in the face. He stopped short in his impulse and interrupted the encounter. The beautiful courtesan, surprised and perhaps a little offended, asked him whether he had seen a physical defect in her. "None," the wise man replied, and affirmed that she was the most beautiful woman he had ever seen. "But," he said, "there is a commandment that is called Tzitzit . . ." He then returned to the study hall (from the Babylon Talmud, Menachot 44a).

The fringes had slapped his face and hidden the naked woman, thus averting his sexual desire, and bringing him back to his studies. The Talmudic story has a double happy end: not only does the rabbi return to the Torah thanks to the tallith, but the beautiful courtesan, following this episode, decides to go and find her client on the other side of the oceans. She marries this man, who thus makes "an honest woman" of her, while he is thus able to "legally" satisfy his desire. Such is the recompense, the passage concludes, of those who respect the *tzitzit* commandment. In this story, which tends towards caricature, the garment is the man's salvation from his misguided senses, and it brings him back to the sensuality of the law; but most of all it is what transforms a purely "consumerist" relationship with a woman into a long-lasting erotic marriage.

This rabbinical text is not a naive or puritanical condemnation of prostitution. Indeed, several sages in the Talmud are clients of sex workers. Nor is it an indictment against sexuality. On the contrary, it reminds us that true intimacy depends on a partially obstructed view and knowledge of others. Accepting that we will not see everything, and that we will not know everything, is what feeds sensuality and desire. And the law must protect rather than censure that desire.

CHAPTER FIVE

Cover That Breast That I Cannot Behold

According to the Israeli newspaper *Haaretz*, a small ultra-orthodox group is now distributing "modesty glasses" in the religious neighbourhoods of Jerusalem.[40] This new gadget is in fact just a simple sticky label you put on the lenses of ordinary glasses. It partially blurs the vision of anyone wearing them, and thus allows its happy owner not to notice the women who cross his path.

The newspaper uses humour to condemn the rising Tartuffe-like religious hypocrisy that has overtaken a certain branch of orthodoxy, while at the same time saluting this initiative in an original way: unlike the segregation some-times imposed on women in buses or in the street, this "ingenious" idea has the merit of imposing no constraints on them at all. The female journalist adds: "If ultra-religious men must not see half of humankind or interact with it, it's a problem. But it's their problem. Let them deal with it. Let them find solutions that limit their own comfort, their

40 August 11, 2012.

own mobility and their ability to act freely in the world, without asking women to go without any of that."

How did the sight of a woman come to be perceived as so dangerous for a handful of ultra-orthodox men? Which texts or traditions have contributed to this visual phobia?

Dangerous visions, dangerous liaisons?

From Genesis onwards, the Bible insists on the danger posed by sight. Eve sees the forbidden fruit and thinks it is beautiful. She then picks it to eat it and give it to Adam. Trouble starts because humanity saw and instantly wanted. This happens in the same way in almost every generation. Noah's son sees his father's nakedness and violates him. Later, Joseph's brothers see the robe his father gave him and tear it off him. The vision of others, in their nakedness or in what covers it, is what causes desire, rivalry and violence.

Throughout Judaism and its rites, there is a great mistrust towards vision and the sense of sight. Regularly presented as likely to turn man from the straight and narrow path, sight is perceived as less reliable than the other senses, notably hearing.

Thus the most central prayer of Judaism, and no doubt the best known, is called the Shema (or Shema Israel). "Shema" literally means "listen". The prayer is an invitation to hear God's commandments and injunctions to his people. The divine word is listened to but not "seen": revelation is auditory first and foremost.

This is what the gestures accompanying the Shema also symbolise: the person saying the prayer is supposed to hide their eyes while reciting the words. They place their hand in front of their eyes to make the obstruction of vision manifest and to recentre themselves on hearing.

At the heart of this same prayer, there is a phrase that is even more explicit than the Torah's warning against sight and its mirages. It is said to the faithful: "Do not stray with your eyes, which will lead you to debauchery." (Numbers 15:39[41]) This is the threat that sight poses: not only can it turn one away from the right path, but it can also, according to the rabbis, lead to sexual debauchery.

What is the connection between sight and prostitution in Judaism? In Hebrew, a prostitute is called a *zona*, a word which has an etymological link with consumption. The words for food (*mazon*) and buffet (*miznon*) derive from the same Hebraic root. The sages of Judaism teach that a prostitute is someone on whom men's eyes feed. In other words, she is a woman who is first consumed through sight.

Prostitution in Hebraic thought is thus linked to sight, inasmuch as it is neither obstructed nor restrained. It is associated with the possibility that an unimpeded view

41 Author's translation.

arouses unlimited desire. It is the result of instantaneous vision, a desire for fulfilment without delay or latency.

Hiding one's eyes in prayer, which is at the heart of the most solemn religious declaration of Judaism, is to voluntarily place a membrane, a filter, between oneself and others. Obstructing one's sight calls forth a relationship to others and the world that is not one of consumption.

The obsession with the liminal zone

Most Jewish rituals mark or determine liminality. They define or signal the transition between two zones, two times, two statuses or two spaces.

For example, the act of lighting the Shabbat candles every Friday night marks the passing from a profane to a sacred time of weekly rest, set apart from the other days of the week. In the same way, each sacred time is inaugurated by a blessing. The passage from one time to another is thus marked by words and ritual, that is, by performative speech. The very meaning of the word "sacred" (*kadosh* in Hebrew) is "set apart". Each of these partitions is associated with a distinguishing gesture.

Jewish rites and identity manifest the centrality of transitions and the importance of celebrating those passages. They almost always seek to recognise crossings and thresholds, and to distinguish the in-between spaces.

Transitions are identified in time and space. Each passage between two places separated by a door is symbolised by a ritual object, the marker of spatial liminality: the mezuzah that separates the interior from the exterior and thus identifies the threshold.

The feast of Pesach, or Passover, is one of the other most notable markers of a passage. This is a time in the Jewish calendar which ritualises a crossing. The story told during Passover is of the passage of the Hebrew people from slavery towards freedom. The founding account of Jewish identity in the Torah is thus a matter of separation. This distinction between two states is what must be acknowledged and commemorated above all else.

Why is it necessary to acknowledge passages? A transition does not need to be marked by anyone in order for it to take place. Life is a series of changes that don't require any acknowledgement for them to occur: each one of us grows old, even if we don't celebrate our birthdays. In the same way, a holiday or a sacred period in the calendar occurs whether anyone lights candles or not, whether anyone has said blessings or not. And yet, the tradition suggests that human involvement modifies the transitions in our lives, not simply as part of the folklore that accompanies them, but in how our words and actions have an impact on reality itself. Human responsibility is involved, making us the guardians of the gates and transitions of our time. These rituals are what John Austin defines as "speech acts". Sentences such as "I declare you husband and wife" or "The court finds you guilty", pronounced in a particular context, constitute not only an utterance but also an act that brings the spoken reality into being. The same applies to religious ritual or liturgy. From the point of view of the tradition, both of these are performative as well.

Jewish law, with its rituals, constantly establishes separations and distinctions. It structures the world by organising its temporality according to contrasting and often antagonistic statuses: profane and sacred times, kosher and non-kosher food, pure and impure states. The passage from one state to the other is rigorously codified.

Judaism thus seems to sound a warning against anything blurred or indeterminate, against any tacit liminality or uncontained porousness. It finds it constantly necessary to point out any grey areas and to establish markers of separation.

Rituals invite us to set a seal on the transitions that mark our lives. By being incarnated in membrane-like rituals, all Jewish rites are experienced as rites of passage, as transitions where humanity is standing in a doorway.

In these rituals we not only acknowledge the passing of time, but also become the agents and witnesses of these crossings.

The sacred veil

The architecture of synagogues provides one of the best illustrations of the art of marked transitions. When you open the door of a synagogue, you generally do not enter directly into a space of prayer. On the contrary, this entrance happens in stages. Several doors must be opened, and an intermediary space passed through, before entering into the centre of the place of worship. A series of thresholds and doorways allow the faithful to slowly approach the heart of prayer. The architecture of synagogues does not allow a direct, unmediated approach to the sacred space.

A synagogue is traditionally constructed like a series of concentric spaces, leading from the profane exterior to the sacred interior. The heart of this sacred space is made material as an ark containing the scrolls of the Torah. The text, sheltered in the very heart of the synagogue, is only taken out for the time of the reading. But most of the time, the Torah remains protected by a cover, and therefore inaccessible to sight. It is placed in a closed space, an ark that is itself separated from the synagogue. This separation is demarcated by a veil, a curtain, in other words: a membrane. The treasure is hidden from sight; access to the sacred is deferred and regulated.

This veil, which in the synagogue separates the congregation from the Torah is a symbolic representation of what occurred in the past when the Temple was in Jerusalem. According to the Bible, at the heart of this place where the divine resides was a sacred space called the Holy of Holies. Tradition has it that nobody could penetrate this space except for one man, the high priest. And even he could only have access to it for a limited time, on the day of Kippur. To enter this space, he would first have to go through the thirteen veils that separated the Holy of Holies from the exterior of the sanctuary.

The Holy of Holies

Let us take a guided tour into the centre of the most sacred place in ancient Judaism. According to the Bible, inside the Holy of Holies was the Ark of the Covenant, containing the Tablets of the Law received on Mount Sinai. This closed Ark was permanently set between its two horizontal carrying staves. Above the entire structure was a sculpture of two winged beings, two angelic figures facing each other above the Ark (Exodus 25:20). When King Solomon inaugurated the Temple, the Ark was installed there with its carrying staves at either end. The biblical text states that, from the outside of the Holy of Holies, an observer could make out these poles, which were visible and invisible at the same time (1 Kings 8:8).

Visible and invisible: this double antonymic qualifier is the source of numerous rabbinic commentaries. How could the carrying staves, in other words the poles, be seen and yet not seen from the exterior of the sanctuary? The Talmud explains that the two staves were so long that they touched the veil of the Holy of Holies, such that they could be seen from the outside of the sacred sanctuary in the form of two protrusions. These two extremities were "seen and yet not seen", and "pushed and protruded and stuck out against the curtain toward the outside". The Talmud describes this spectacle using an unexpected metaphor: the ends of the two poles were like "the two breasts of a woman pushing against her clothes" (Babylon Talmud, Yoma 54a:10).[42]

The most sacred sight of all, that of the Holy of Holies, beheld by those going to the Temple, is described in the Talmud as akin to the sight of almost visible female nudity. In a fleeting vision of a woman's breasts, the religious urge coincides with carnal desire.

When the high priest drew the curtain to briefly expose the interior of the Holy of Holies, he revealed the image of two cherubim sculpted above the Ark, united in a loving embrace.[43]

42 For a discussion of this translation, see Marc-Alain Ouaknin, *The Burnt Book: Reading the Talmud* (Princeton, NJ: Princeton University Press, 1998).
43 Ibid.

In the sacred space, the only image available to the people is a carnal vision: a woman's breasts, or an erotic coupling. Neither unwholesome nor reprehensible, this image is on the contrary consecrated and religious. The curtain of the Holy of Holies suggests, but does not show completely. It is a membrane that allows the vision of the sacred.

Desire and sacredness have in common the necessity of a play of veils, which is the only means of looking at what is not directly visible. What is consecrated is thus deferred, indirect sight, rather than the immediate sight of the object approached, desired, but never won.

This idea of a veil being necessary for sight is found in many other cultures. Plato's allegory of the cave evokes it in its own way, by suggesting that one cannot perceive things or ideas directly. Humans are prisoners of their dark environments, and cannot, without effort or science, see anything but their shadows on the wall of the cave. Ideas, just like what is sacred, are not accessible without mediation. It is impossible to have a direct relationship with, or a non-mediated view of, what is fundamental. In order to perceive it, humans need veils that act as filters and translate the infinite into the finite. Such is the modesty of the infinite: it never lets itself be seen naked. Or more accurately, none of us can behold it naked.

For Judaism, this language of the sacred is a language of the flesh. Neither visible nor representable, the divine is "translated" into the forms of a female body, or metonymically into a part of her anatomy. This idea of a carnal and female projection of the divine recurs throughout several Talmudic texts, and in the Bible itself.

God is sometimes called El Shaddai, an expression that can be literally translated as "God of the breasts". The metaphor of the breast, in its maternal function, is repeated throughout rabbinical literature: sometimes to describe the Torah, which feeds its offspring – namely those who study it[44] – and sometimes to present the heroes of the Bible. A case in point: Moses and his brother Aaron are compared in some rabbinical legends to "a woman's breasts: one is not bigger than the other" (Shir Hashirim Rabba 4:12). Both are capable of nourishing the people with their wisdom, of breastfeeding them with their knowledge.

It is important not to reduce these kinds of metaphors found in the scriptures to their literal meanings. Of course, God is not a woman, and women are not divine. To confuse the transcendent with one of its translations created by men is blasphemous, for such an act would make an idol of the divine by reducing it to a gender. It is, however, worth considering the meaning of the female projection of the divine, particularly in a world where the place women occupy is so limited.

44 See Isaiah 66:10–11 – a verse traditionally interpreted as the Torah being able to "breastfeed" those who seek consolation there.

Excess "textosterone"

For a long time, the scriptures of the three Abrahamic religions were read, edited and commented upon only by men. One might well wonder whether the metaphors and language of the texts would have been different if their readers were men *and* women. The exclusively male interpretation perhaps explains, in part, why whatever is sacred appears in the literature with feminine characteristics. Philosophy, another temple that has long been exclusively male, often does much the same with its metaphors for transcendence. Friedrich Nietzsche, in *The Joyous Science*, describes sacred truth as a veiled woman "who has reasons for not showing her reasons".[45]

Contemporary readers of the source texts, no matter what their views, must take the identity of the generations of interpreters into account, along with the ways their metaphors have been shaped by their world views and how our world allows us to grasp them now.

What would sacredness and truth look like, if women had been allowed to join their voices to the commentaries? Are the literary images of the inaccessible feminine absolute a simple reflection of the gender of their authors? Do these readings suffer from what Rabbi Naama Kalman calls

45 Friedrich Nietzsche, *The Joyous Science*, tr. and ed. R. Kevin Hill (London: Penguin Classics, 2018), p. 23.

"excess textosterone"? Or rather, do femininity and its symbols provide the only language capable of putting what is sacred and mysterious into words, for both men and women? Is the female gender one of mystery and transcendence for everyone?

The man who wore a veil

In Judaism, with its non-incarnated divine, veiling is a way to make the inaccessible accessible, the invisible visible. It allows us to perceive what is disincarnate and infinite, beyond the material boundaries of the world.

The Christian scriptures take up this idea in a remarkable way. According to Christian tradition, when Jesus died, the veil covering the Holy of Holies in the Temple was torn. The Christian God, once incarnated, made veiling the divine superfluous, since the divine had at last revealed itself. But for Judaism, the divine remains what cannot be seen; it is by definition the impossible vision, the one referred to in the Bible when it says: "You cannot see My face, for man may not see Me and live" (Exodus 33:20). Every man?

The only being in the Jewish tradition who is not subject to this law is Moses, the only human who saw God and lived. In the Bible, he is the only one who ever faces the divine, on the summit of Mount Sinai. However, when he descends from the mountain, this encounter seems to have mysteriously changed his appearance: according to the scripture, Moses' face is then "radiant" (Exodus 34:30).

After this irradiating face-to-face encounter with the divine, Moses appears to be contaminated, his skin is flayed to the quick. The scripture states that from that moment on he will wear a veil to speak to the people. It has become impossible for him to speak with his skin bare, without a membrane or a veil, to those who are incapable of perceiving the infinite and of approaching the divine as he did.

Moses must be veiled in order to unveil to others what he learns from God. He acts as a filter for the people, reducing the intensity and luminosity of the divine to make these features perceptible. He is the one who, in the text, incarnates the paradox of revelation: the need to hide in order to reveal. His veil is not needed to hide something, but acts as an intermediary between the finite and the infinite. It is because he has been too close to the divine that he must now cover himself when he goes out.

It is important to note here that traditional religious discourse generally calls for women to be covered, not men.

Is the feminine condition, like Moses, closer to the divine? Is demanding that a woman be veiled or covered akin to recognising that she enjoys greater proximity to the divine and the infinite? Does this suggest that a woman's unveiled skin exposes a man to a greater radiance than he can stand?

Whether women take pride in this implied proximity to the divine or not, we must remain lucid: the sacralisation of the feminine condition is always an elegant prelude to women's social marginalisation.

CHAPTER SIX

The Orificial Being

In Judaism, in principle, men and women do meet. Celibacy
is never elevated into a virtue. In fact, it is often condemned
by the rabbis of the Talmud. Judaism cannot be defined as
an ascetic religion. While a few small groups have sometimes adopted this philosophy during Judaism's long history,
this has never been a norm in Jewish thought. Sexual pleasure and fulfilment are not condemned: on the contrary,
they are sometimes a matter of duty. Some commentators
even assert that God judges each man not only for his
transgressions during his life, but also for what he didn't
do when he was allowed to.[46] Jewish practice does not laud
excessive restraint, which it even tends to find suspect.
Asceticism is never a community matter, with the notable
exception of one day per year: Yom Kippur.

*

46 See the Jerusalem Talmud, Kiddushin 48b: "Rabbi Hezkiya, Rabbi Cohen
in the name of Rav: In the future, a person will give a judgement and an
accounting over everything that his eye saw and he did not eat."

Every year, on the Day of Atonement, Jews gather together in great numbers at the synagogue. The liturgy on this day of fasting makes reference to divine judgement, human introspection and forgiveness. During more than twenty-four hours, tradition invites the faithful to a form of asceticism, with no food or drink, with no entertainment or trivial conversation, no trading or sexual activity. These hours of prayer are considered a kind of "training" for one's own death, a conditioning exercise for the day of the Last Judgement.

In the middle of the afternoon of fasting, when hunger is making itself felt and tiredness begins to grow heavy, the faithful read an extract from the Torah at the synagogue, taken from the book of Leviticus, which has the effect of adding the psychological discomfort of its topic to their existing physical discomfort. The passage is a long list of sexual interdicts, in the heart of which are incestuous relations. In particular:

> None of you shall come near anyone of his own flesh to uncover nakedness: I am the LORD. Your father's nakedness, that is, the nakedness of your mother, you shall not uncover; she is your mother – you shall not uncover her nakedness. Do not uncover the nakedness of your father's wife; it is the nakedness of your father. The nakedness of your sister – your father's daughter

or your mother's, whether born into the household or outside – do not uncover their nakedness. The nakedness of your son's daughter, or of your daughter's daughter – do not uncover their nakedness; for their nakedness is yours. The nakedness of your father's wife's daughter, who was born into your father's household – she is your sister; do not uncover her nakedness. Do not uncover the nakedness of your father's sister; she is your father's flesh. Do not uncover the nakedness of your mother's sister; for she is your mother's flesh. Do not uncover the nakedness of your father's brother: do not approach his wife; she is your aunt. Do not uncover the nakedness of your daughter-in-law: she is your son's wife; you shall not uncover her nakedness. Do not uncover the nakedness of your brother's wife; it is the nakedness of your brother. [Leviticus 18:6–16]

This long passage lists the sexual interdicts like a leitmotif. The exhortation not to "uncover the nakedness" of a number of relatives, whose precise personal or family status is given and whose closeness or physical condition makes them unapproachable, is repeated over and over.

In the Bible, the expression "uncovered nakedness" is always a euphemism for sexual relations. But in rabbinical literature, this expression (*gilui arayot* in Hebrew) has come to describe a particular kind of sexuality: incestuous relationships. This intimacy, with someone who is too close or the legitimate partner of a close relation, is the most forbidden intimacy of all. The nakedness of another person's wife is described, by transposition, as the nakedness of that other person ("the nakedness of your father's wife [. . .] is the nakedness of your father").

It may seem surprising that this passage has been included in the liturgy of the most solemn day in the Jewish calendar. How are we to understand the fact that sexual interdicts should be an integral part of the ritual, precisely on the day when all sexual activity is forbidden, and when asceticism is upheld? Maybe on a day devoted to family reunions the purpose is to mark the sacred and inviolable nature of family relationships, to remind the faithful what constitutes the prohibition of incest in our communities? The purpose is to reaffirm the sacred foundations of community living, and to celebrate what Claude Lévi-Strauss called "the fundamental step because of which, by which, but above all in which, the transition from nature to culture is accomplished".[47]

47 *The Elementary Structures of Kinship*, tr. James Harle Bell, John Richard von Sturmer and Rodney Needham (Boston, MA: Beacon Press, 1969), p. 24.

Secrets and secretions

The nakedness that must not be uncovered has a particular name in Leviticus: *erva*. This word, repeated in each verse like a mantra, also refers to the genital area. Its etymology is surprising enough to warrant attention. In order to understand the Hebrew word *erva*, it is worth studying the words that derive from the same Hebrew root.

In the Bible, this term usually refers to the genital organs, both male and female. But the root of the word is found in several other meanings, which might initially seem quite remote. Many occurrences relate to the flow of fluid, to the action of emptying or pouring out a liquid,[48] whether this is water or blood.[49] The root of the word *erva* is thus linked to both the sexual organs and the flowing of a liquid.

Moreover, some biblical expressions use it in a different sense altogether. In Deuteronomy, it is said that a man can repudiate his wife if he finds "*ervat davar*", or literally "a fact of *erva*",[50] an expression that is translated as "unseemliness", or "weakness". *Erva* also sometimes means vulnerability.[51] In

48 See also in Genesis 24:20, *Ta'er*: Rebecca "empties water" into the drinking trough.
49 See Ezekiel 16:22. *Eria* (same root) means "flowing blood".
50 Deuteronomy 24:1.
51 See Genesis 42:9 and Isaiah 20:4: Joseph's brothers are accused of coming to explore "*ervat haaretz*", the vulnerability of Egypt. Sefaria translates this as "the nakedness of the land".

these different uses, the same word thus correlates to a fault or a fissure.

In summary, the word describes in turn the genital organs, nakedness, flowing or a fissure. By bringing together these various uses of the word, it becomes clear that this Hebrew root always has something to do with an orifice, or a fissure from which a liquid may flow. It refers to a secret place, or a place that secretes. In French and English, these two words also have a common etymology: "secretion" and "secret" both come from the same Latin word *secretio* ("separation").

In order to understand the deeper meaning of the word *erva*, we need to consider the physiological phenomenon of secretion. Biologically, this notion refers to the capacity of living tissue, an organ, or a cell to discharge a substance outside itself. The site of the secretion is thus the point where the inside and outside meet, where there is a passage through a membrane or a tissue.

The best translation, as I see it, of the word *erva* is thus a "zone of secretion", a site of passage from the interior to the exterior of a tissue or a body. That which is hidden becomes visible. That which is secret is unveiled and what is dissimulated is laid bare. Shmuel Trigano defines this as "what lets itself be totally exposed in its exteriority, while it is in fact associated with interiority".[52]

52 *Le Judaïsme et l'Esprit du monde* (Judaism and the Spirit of the World) (Paris: Grasset, 2012), p. 151.

The issue this discovery raises is again one of direct visibility, in other words, the unmediated exposure of what was previously hidden. A membrane of separation is crossed, torn or made porous, and the border between the inside and the outside of the body is thus blurred.

To discover *erva*, the interdict repeated in Leviticus, is to cross the membrane and to know what should remain secret, to see what should be hidden.

From nudity in general to women's nudity in particular

It is worth noting that there is some slippage in the meaning of the term *erva* between its use in the Bible and in later rabbinical writings. Whereas in the Bible the term was applied to men's nakedness as well as to women's, in the later texts (the Talmud, rabbinical legends, etc.) it gradually comes to qualify only female sexual organs or anything to do with feminine nudity or sexuality. In other words, whereas in the Bible all humankind is naked, over time only woman-kind remains so.

A similar slippage is also at work in the case of the Arabic word *farj*. In the beginning, this term designated men's and women's sexual organs, then it came to refer only to women's. According to Fethi Benslama, who provides evidence for this in "Le Sexuel monothéiste et sa traduction scientifique" (Monotheistic sexuality and its scientific translations), "a fall therefore occurs inside the discourse, a 'symbolic lesion of the word', to use Jacques Lacan's expression, through which the notion of sex disappears, and in a particular way, since only the woman has it, in terms of her sexual organs".[53] Gradually, nudity becomes entirely feminine.

A second slippage in the historical meaning of *erva*, with significant consequences, occurs later. Having first qualified the sexual organs in general and then specifically women's sexual organs, the term *erva* in rabbinical literature gradually comes to mean the numerous female body parts whose exposure is considered potentially sexually suggestive. Any uncovered part that is likely to cause emotion in the man who sees or hears it is defined as nakedness. In the Talmud, a woman's voice is thus qualified as nakedness, as is her hair or any parts of her skin that might stimulate desire when exposed.

Women thus become beings who are almost entirely "*erva*-genic": secret and secreting beings whose surface, like a mucous membrane, betrays the interior of their bodies. If we now consider the term *erva* as synonymous with a secreting membrane, a zone of juncture between the inside and outside of the body, it appears then that women are beings

53 In *Cliniques Méditerranéennes*, 73 (2006), pp. 89–95.

with no skin. They have much less exterior surface at their disposal than men do, since large stretches of their anatomy (legs, hair, etc.) are paradoxically considered part of their interiority. The mucus-woman is too porous or too see-through to be able to hide the inside of her body.

Donkey skin – woman's skin

Demanding that a woman cover herself thus consists of an attempt to create an exterior membrane, in other words to place a second skin on what is perceived as overexposed intimacy. A secret that has become too visible must be modestly covered up.

In the land of fairy tales, where princesses must hide to escape the curses that threaten them, the woman needs protection from a skin or a coat, for her body is too naked to be exposed without danger. In "Donkey-Skin", the fairy tale by Charles Perrault, a widowed king decides to marry his daughter, whose skin is fair and fine, and whose beauty is matchless in his entire kingdom. In order to escape from her father's murky incestuous plans, the princess listens to the advice of her fairy godmother, who tells her to get hold of the skin of the royal donkey. Covered in this horrible animal coat, she is at last able to leave the palace and to escape her father's desire. The princess's naked skin makes her vulnerable, prey to father's sexual violence. Her second skin covers and protects her, because it makes her ugly. This is the only way she is able to get away from the palace.

In Perrault's tale, the woman is threatened because she is naked. As is, along with her, the entire moral order of a whole society where the interdict of incest is unstable. Once she is covered, the woman is no longer an object of men's irrepressible desire. It's almost as if she was instantaneously neutralised by the animal identity she takes on, which seems to counterbalance her fragile femininity. The fairy tells her: "Wrap yourself in this skin, leave the palace, and walk so long as you can find ground to carry you: when one sacrifices everything to virtue the gods know how to mete out reward."[54] Thanks to her donkey skin, the woman can now exist outside herself, and outside the palace, just like a man. And with good reason: the skin is that of a male donkey, and because the male is the being endowed with skin, he can go outside without danger. The mucus-woman, who is far too vulnerable, remains condemned to inhabit her interiority, inside her hymen, unless a grafted skin allows her to no longer threaten the world with her immodesty. The body of the animal is subjected to violence, so that the woman's body is not. The animal loses its skin so the woman can have one at last.

54 Charles Perrault, "Donkey-Skin", from *The Fairy Tales of Charles Perrault*, tr. Robert Samber and J. E. Mansion (London: Harrap, 1922), p. 147.

The impure woman

If immodesty is the exposure of what should remain inside, it becomes clear why so many texts in rabbinical literature are concerned with the body's secretions, and particularly with women's flows.

During part of her cycle, around the time of menstruation, a woman is considered *niddah* in Jewish law, which means she is "kept apart". Some forms of contact with a menstruating woman are forbidden, notably sexual relations. Her state is generally described as a transitory situation of impurity. But the term "impurity" (the translation of the Hebrew *tumah*) is both complex and disturbing. In order to understand its meaning, we need to refer to other situations that create a similar state, according to Jewish law. A man who has an involuntary emission of sperm, or "nocturnal pollution", is also considered to be in a similar state for a restricted time. After childbirth, a woman has the same status. She is considered untouchable, and temporarily kept apart from the group.

The common feature of these very different situations is the reference to emissions or secretion, in other words the passage of an interior "product" to the exterior, from the invisible domain to the visible. Impurity is therefore seen as a form of excess exposure, a bodily flaw, which necessitates a temporary distancing of the person involved, to give them the time to reconstitute their "boundaries" in this state of isolation. The overexposed body is, for a time, "dis-exposed".

The concept of impurity, in our societies and to the modern mind, is both subversive and abstract. It is associated with being dirty, or soiled. In Hebrew, its origin is more complex. A Jewish text from the eleventh century CE defines three major sources of impurity: death, leprosy and reptiles (Tahorot 1:5). This restricted list deserves to be decrypted. The three scourges cited each have something to do with a borderline state of decomposition. In each case, a membrane between the inside and the outside disappears or is no longer clear.

Leprosy is a skin illness associated with its most visible symptoms, the decomposition of the dermis, in other words the destruction of a frontier between the inside and outside of the body. The snake is the animal that naturally and frequently experiences the same desquamation, the one that moults and loses its exterior membrane. And finally, death, from a biological point of view, is often defined as the moment that the membranes of physiological separations cease to function. The life of cells is assured by the existence of barriers that separate the tissues and organs, and which create tension or a difference in pressure on either side of the separation. What defines life is notably the imbalance in pressure on one side and the other of a membrane. A living organism is in a state of non-homeostasis: the difference in pressure enables the passage of elements from one side of the membrane to the other, whereas death puts an end to that pressure and pulsation.

The decomposition of membranes is thus the feature common to all three of these phenomena. This may be, in Hebraic thought, the source of impurity. A body is impure when it no longer presents a clear separation between its inside and outside, between what is hidden within it and what is visible.

Described as a nakedness, or *erva*, a woman's body, including her hair and her voice, would thus be considered an intimate zone even on its surface. Considering a woman's body to be similar to a mucous membrane is to see it as more porous than a man's, as covered with a much more fragile and transparent membrane than the male body is. According to this point of view, women are beings made of membranes that split apart or come unstuck. In some sense, womanhood is assimilated to the menstrual process.

Women are also strongly associated with the physiology of motherhood and life in the womb. They are the ones who open themselves up to give life, the ones whose bodies become the passage between the inside and the outside. The rupture of a membrane allows for birth, but it also leads to death. Women are thus an open door between one side and the other, between the inside and the outside, between the invisible and the revealed, between life and death.

The word for "feminine" or "female" in Hebrew is *nekeva*, which literally means "a hole". In the scriptures, women are often the pierced beings, the orificial beings.

What if the fear of femininity was first and foremost to do with this: a fear of the abolition of membranes, the phenomenon that biologically defines death? The demand for modesty would then consist in re-establishing the borders, rehabilitating that separation in order to keep death at a distance, along with women.

The body, a social microcosm

In *Purity and Danger*, the anthropologist Mary Douglas suggests that the bodily rituals of a given society are always the reflection of the perception of the social body. She writes that the body is always the symbolic carrier of the social organisation in which it lives. "The powers and dangers credited to social structure [are] reproduced in small on the human body."[55] In other words, it is always the mirror of the universe, of which it becomes the microcosm.

If we assume that the fear of femininity might, in some religious literature, have something to do with the understanding of the body as porous, the obsession with women's

55 Mary Douglas, *Purity and Danger: An Analysis of Concepts of Pollution and Taboo* (London: Routledge, 1966), p. 116.

modesty may be linked to the group's anxiety about its social limits. A member of the community is considered too vulnerable to be exposed. Is this perhaps an incarnation of the necessity to protect other vulnerable attributes of the group, namely its membranes? Exposing the group without protecting it would run the risk of social contamination in its liminal zones.

Examining notions of modesty brings us to question the less overt underlying criteria of belonging to the group: who is inside? Who is excluded? Who protects the borders? Who threatens them? Perhaps the obsession with covering the female body is a translation of the concern about the porosity of the group. Exposed nakedness reflects the membrane separating the group from its environment and threatens its impermeability.

CHAPTER SEVEN

Man, a Woman Like Any Other?

How fair you are, how beautiful! O Love,
with all its rapture! Your stately form
is like the palm, your breasts are
like clusters [of fruit].
Song of Songs 7:7–8

The Bible is mistrustful of nakedness, with the exception of one book that praises it. The Song of Songs resounds like an erotic poem, a biblical love song. Its eight chapters describe a man and a woman searching for love, who seek and desire, court and then miss each other. They hope to find each other again, but never do. Throughout the account, the tension in their loving relationship feeds their unfulfilled desire. This search for the other, a magnificent hymn of desire, never speaks explicitly about God, or faith, or religion. On the surface, there is nothing there about theology or religiosity. And yet this text is the one which in the Jewish tradition becomes the very quintessence of sacred literature, a keystone of the biblical canon. In the second century BCE, a celebrated sage of the Talmud, Rabbi Akiba, affirms: "All the writings are holy, but the Song of Songs is the holy of holies" (Mishnah Yadayim 3:5).

Jewish commentators have given this poem allegorical readings: the man is God himself and his beloved is God's people; the link between the divine and man is shown metaphorically through this tense relationship between lovers. The connection is presented as desire and union. Christianity later also considers this loving relationship as a projection of what connects Jesus to his Church.

This allegory is surprising because of its paradoxical nature: how can it be that in the world of the yeshiva, of the synagogue or the church, a world from which women are traditionally kept apart, an erotic relationship between a man and a woman should serve as a model for access to the divine? This rhetorical device is even more surprising in that the group of male readers identifies itself not with the man, but in fact with the woman in the text.

Femininity, which one might think was peripheral or negligible in a largely androcentric literary universe, seems on the contrary to be surprisingly present in description of the community of the faithful. Men constantly read and study scriptures that treat them as the women of God. In the religious world, women are often kept at a distance, but femininity is often laid claim to. This paradox between rejection and appropriation is what we will now explore.

Man as wife of the divine

In the love story of God and his people Israel, the divine is often presented in the scriptures as a jealous husband choosing for himself a companion with the features of a feminine "chosen" people.

The Bible and subsequent rabbinical literature cultivate an image of the relationship with the divine as a marriage, and often use the extended metaphor of the wedding. The gift of the Torah on Mount Sinai, in the episode where the people gathered at the foot of the mountain to receive the Tablets of the Law, is often described as a wedding ceremony. Israel is a bride preparing herself for the encounter with her beloved, to seal a covenant with him. The Tablets of the Law are the marriage contract that the bridegroom offers his future wife, while all creation and the angels are witnesses to this union whose nuptial canopy is the celestial vault. The divine bridegroom makes an alliance with his people, who engage themselves to establish a faithful relationship, in other words, not to "betray" him with other gods.

*

In the Bible and Jewish literature of the first centuries CE, the people of Israel are often given feminine characteristics, and God weaves an intimate relationship with them and fulfils all their needs. Thus, in the words of the prophet Ezekiel, God addresses his people to remind them of the blessed moment of their loving encounter: "When I passed by you [again] and saw that your time for love had arrived. So I spread My robe over you and covered your nakedness, and I entered into a covenant with you by oath – declares the Lord GOD; thus you became Mine" (16:8).

But the honeymoon period and blissful love are ephemeral. The people of Israel are later often presented as an unreliable and fickle wife. The relationship is then condemned to go through many crises.

The wife-people appear incapable of resisting the call of other potential lovers, of other gods: this is the temptation of polytheism or idolatry. Israel straying from the path of monotheism is always described in the Bible through the metaphor of adultery, of a depraved and unfaithful wife, who is prepared to forget her conjugal commitments.

In the book of Ezekiel, God laments this: "But confident in your beauty and fame, you played the harlot: you lavished your favours on every passerby; they were his" (16:15).

However, of the whole biblical canon the book of Hosea is undoubtedly the most explicit about this. This is the story of a prophet who takes a prostitute as a wife and builds a home with her. The couple, who split and fall apart, become a metaphor for what threatens God's relationship with his people. Despite the woman's debauchery and depravity, Hosea receives the order from God to take her again as his legitimate wife. This book of the Bible can be considered an allegory for the damaged but repairable connection between God and his people, like a relationship that suffers from the treachery and debauchery of a woman. Its message is that, just as Hosea was able to bring the one he loved back to the path of a virtuous marriage, God has not lost confidence in his people.

God finally declares to his people, who have come back to him: "And I will espouse you forever: I will espouse you with righteousness and justice, and with goodness and mercy, and I will espouse you with faithfulness; then you shall be devoted to the LORD" (Hosea 2:21–2). These two verses of marital reconciliation at the heart of the book of Hosea are perfectly known by all observant Jews, since they are recited almost every morning in prayer.

Taking a wife, every morning

Almost every day, practising Jews wind leather straps called phylacteries or tefillin around their arms and foreheads. On each of these bands is a little box containing a scroll of parchment covered in scriptures. These prayer accessories are put on daily, almost like a tiara and bracelets. The man winds the straps around himself and dons the scriptures like jewellery that envelops him (traditionally only men wear tefillin, although some women in the liberal Jewish world now do so too).

The leather bands are wrapped around the arms and attached to the hands, like a ring around a finger. At the precise moment when the man winds the strap around his middle finger, as he would put on an engagement ring, he pronounces the verse from Hosea about God espousing his people.

Men repeat the words of the bridegroom-God to his people daily. The act of putting on tefillin, which opens morning prayers, includes a scene of marriage in its words and gestures. God's word addressed to men is a promise of love repeated daily to those who adorn themselves with it like a jewel.

Here again in this allegorical evocation, the divine bridegroom is male, whereas the man praying is symbolically female. The verse from Hosea addresses a woman: in Hebrew, the interlocutor is grammatically feminine.

There are other moments in Jewish worship when the man seems feminised in this way, notably on the day of a ritual which, by definition, only pertains to males: circumcision.

On the day of his entry into the covenant, the little boy, usually eight days old, is held on his godfather's knees during the ablation of his foreskin that marks in his flesh his identification with the group. The liturgy spoken during the ceremony comes in part from the book of Ezekiel. It is said repeatedly to the male child at the moment when a little blood flows from his penis: "You will live in your blood!" (Ezekiel 16:6). This mysterious verse refers to the passage in the Bible when God comes to the rescue of his wounded beloved, protects her, and creates a covenant with her. The "you" of the verse, addressed to the infant, is once again grammatically formulated in the feminine. It is in the feminine that the male baby is addressed upon his entry into the covenant.

Why should a language addressed exclusively to males be feminised? There are conflicting interpretations about this apparent "confusion" of genders in the ritual. In a book entitled *Sex of the Soul*, Charles Mopsik suggests that circumcision symbolically serves to get rid of any ambiguity about the sexual belonging of the little boy.[56] Once he has left a woman's body, the male child must be differentiated from his original state, severed from where he comes from, the female, in order to permanently distinguish himself from it. According to this theory, the foreskin is identified as a female organ, like a membrane characteristic of female anatomy, of which he must rid himself in order to enter into real and definitive masculinity. At the instant of circumcision, the little boy then enters into the world of men for ever, by getting rid of a skin that, like a hymen, connects him to the world of women. We considered in our last chapter the idea that femaleness is defined as a site of passage between the inside and the outside of the body. The male sexual organ, once it is rid of this membrane, becomes entirely exterior, in other words it becomes male with no possible ambiguity.

According to other researchers, circumcision is precisely the reverse process. The cutting symbolises a form of partial feminisation of the body of the little boy, through the inscription in the male flesh of a "deficiency" seen as radically feminine.[57] In Hebrew, the word for "feminine" is *nekeva*, which, in addition to "hole", can also mean "pierced"

---

56 *Sex of the Soul: The Vicissitudes of Sexual Difference in Kaballah* (Los Angeles: Cherub Press, 2005).

57 Daniel Boyarin, "This We Know to Be the Carnal Israel: Circumcision and the Erotic Life of God and Israel", *Critical Inquiry*, 18/3 (1992), pp. 474–505.

or "obliterated", and refers to the existence of a lack in the flesh. According to this view, circumcision incarnates this obliteration and inscribes it in the body. Entering into a covenant with the divine thus signifies being ready to enter into an enduring feminine–masculine relationship with God, and preparing oneself for a religious life similar to a marriage.

The feminine posture in which the Jewish man presents himself is apparently not problematic for rabbis. The people of Israel are the wife of the divine in the Bible, and Jewish men, individually, are also placed in a relationship with it as wives of God. Gilles-Avraham Morali writes in *Kabbale, corps et âme* (Kabbalah, body and soul) that "the greatness of Israel, as a being, is knowing that it is only the feminine of God", the female partner of the divine.[58]

Howard Eilberg-Schwartz, in *God's Phallus*, cites numerous extracts of rabbinical literature from the first centuries CE where a biblical hero is deprived of a masculine attribute, or placed in a feminising situation, in order to elevate himself.[59] Referring to medieval commentaries, he cites the account of Jacob wrestling with the angel, when the patriarch is wounded at the top of his thigh, near the hip,

58 Gilles-Avraham Morali, *Kabbale, corps et âme* (Kaballah, Body and Soul) (Villeurbanne: Éditions Ramhal, 2009), p. 90.
59 Howard Eilberg-Schwartz, *God's Phallus and Other Problems for Men and Monotheism* (Boston, MA: Beacon Press, 1994).

and considers this wound to be connected to the sexual organ.[60] In the biblical euphemism, Jacob is wounded in the hip and almost emasculated at the very moment when he acquires the name "Israel", which he will pass down to his descendants.

In a text dating to the tenth century (Tanna Debei Eliyahu Rabbah), the expulsion of Adam from the Garden of Eden is told in the form of a repudiation of a wife by her husband. In this account, God gives Adam a *get* (a religious divorce) as he leaves Eden, just as a man does to the woman from whom he separates. In this text, it is thus the entirety of humanity, and not only the Jewish people, which is treated by God as a woman. The expulsion from Eden makes each one of us a repudiated wife.

Worship and childcare

In some ways, the rituals of Jewish worship also represent this feminisation of the faithful, within the enclosure of the synagogue. In Jewish orthodox communities, men and women are separated. Men occupy the main space and

60   The anatomical part that is affected is called the "nashe" tendon. Etymologically, this is connected with the Hebrew word for women "nashim". The celebrated commentator Rashi suggests that Jacob was wounded near the organ of the covenant, the *brit mila*.

conduct the service, while women are seated in a more peripheral space, either above the place of prayer – on the balcony – or behind the scenes, in the "chicken coop". The women are separated from the masculine space by a low wall or a curtain, called a *mehitza* ("cut") in Hebrew.

The men, who lead the service, are in charge of the reading of the Torah. The ceremony of taking out the parchments in synagogues is highly choreographed and ritualised. At a precise moment in the liturgy, all the faithful stand up and the curtain of the ark is opened. The rolls of the Torah appear and one of them is gently placed in the arms of a man from the congregation who embraces it almost like a parent holding a child against his shoulder. The man and the book he is thus lovingly carrying then start a procession through the main space of the synagogue, in other words exclusively among the men present. It is traditional for each of these men to approach the roll throughout the ritual of procession, to touch it gently, or to kiss the cloth covering it. Sometimes the roll is passed from hand to hand, but it is always handled with great care and tenderness. At the end of the procession, the man and the Torah return to the altar, where the Torah can be undressed and read.

During the procession, the book is shown the greatest possible respect. It is carried like a baby being presented to a community, whose members draw near to pamper and kiss it. Later on in the service, the roll is held aloft, carried high in the air, and presented so that all can see it, like a newborn baby being welcomed by the extended family, the gathered tribe.

This image of a community doting on its scriptures like a parent on a child is carried through into the reading ritual. The clothing of the Torah, made of a precious fabric, is delicately removed, revealing another cloth called a *mappah*, a long band of cotton or linen wrapped around the parchment itself. This cloth wrapping could be described as a kind of "underwear" for the Torah. And it is, literally, since what envelops the scriptures is in fact a baby's swaddling cloth. In the Ashkenazi Jewish tradition, a boy of three years old customarily brings one of his baby cloths to the synagogue, in the form of a long piece of fabric. This cloth, embroidered by his mother or grandmother, bears his name, sometimes his date of birth and the names of his parents. This is the cloth that will then be wound around the Torah. Thus the book, the beloved child of the community, is clothed in the garment of a child, who is also protected and cared for by his parents.

The sacred rite of reading the Torah, traditionally reserved for men in the enclosure of the synagogue, looks somewhat like pampering a baby. In some ways the ceremony mimics motherhood, or at least the gestures that were once the preserve of mothers, in a man's world from which women are excluded or are mere spectators.

In fact, real mothers are kept at a distance from these rituals, isolated on the other side of a barrier. Daniel Boyarin offers an original interpretation of this exclusion. He talks about what he calls the rabbis' couvade, which he analyses as a male desire for, or jealousy of, certain female attributes. Men symbolically appropriate certain functions within the liturgy that they do not (or did not) undertake outside the walls of the synagogue.[61]

This is antithetical to the famous Freudian theory of penis envy, where women are the ones who are jealous of the organ they don't possess. Here, in Boyarin's definition of a couvade, it is the men who try to appropriate what they lack. Men are the ones who perceive themselves as defective, whereas women present themselves as entire and fulfilled. Men's religious activities are seen as their desire for maternity, which is not so much a celebration of women as an attempt to appropriate and control feminine and maternal functions.

Men with periods

Many cultures habitually feminise their enemies, thereby presenting them as weak or degenerate. These attacks on the virility of the opponent are found as frequently among

61 Daniel Boyarin, "Jewish Masochism: Couvade, Castration and Rabbis in Pain", *American Imago*, 51 (1994), pp. 3–36.

spectators at sports events as they are in the ranks of armies. The enemies of a nation or a group are often judged to be "effeminate" by their adversaries.

The Jews have been particular victims of this denigrating, gendered discourse throughout history. There are numerous anti-Semitic writings from the Middle Ages about Jewish bodies and their supposedly deviant physiology. One of the characteristics attributed to Jewish men in these texts is that they have monthly periods, just like women. In fact, it is this theory that was used to justify the persistent accusations of ritual murder: some anti-Semitic writings suggest that monthly bleeding leads Jewish men to attack Christian children, in order to regenerate the blood they lose during menstruation.[62]

In the Middle Ages, numerous religious texts, whether Christian or Jewish, described women's menstruation as a punishment meted out to each new generation for Eve's sin, a kind of hereditary curse resulting from the original act of transgression. Medieval anti-Semitic Christian literature extrapolates this idea: if periods are the punishment for original sin, the Jews, both men and women, must also pay

62   See for example *Acta Sanctorum*, Vol. 2, April 1675, section 507, where Gottfried Henschen explains that "Jewish men and women suffer from menstrual bleeding. They have discovered that drinking Christian blood is an effective treatment for this complaint."

by bleeding for their own "original sin", that of not recognising the real God.[63]

Sander Gilman, in *The Jew's Body*, affirms that Jewish masculinity was already perceived in Greco-Roman times as feminised.[64] One of the elements of this non-virile image is the rite of circumcision, which was seen as castration by the Greeks and Romans, who abhorred this practice.

This non-virile masculinity, which was present in Greek and Christian anti-Semitic rhetoric, was in some ways reclaimed by the Jews themselves as their own. Not as a failing, a curse or a weakness, but, on the contrary, as a distinction. It was seen as an elevation above the brutal and bestial virility which, according to rabbinical literature, Rome perfectly incarnated.

In the Talmud, there is a recurring rhetoric that celebrates the Jewish man, and particularly his rabbinical archetype, as different and superior to the hyper-masculine machismo of the Roman world. Jewish masculinity becomes a counter-model to that of the gladiators; the Jewish ethos of virility is thus a reaction to the markers and attributes of Roman virility in the environment of the time. Because Roman culture abhorred masculine submission, the Jews took it

63 Sander L. Gilman, *Jewish Self-Hatred: Antisemitism and the Hidden Language of the Jews* (Baltimore, MD: Johns Hopkins University Press, 1986), pp. 74–5.
64 Sander L. Gilman, *The Jew's Body* (London: Routledge, 1992).

upon themselves to value it, as a social choice that constituted a form of resistance to the dominant culture. In an environment that valued strength and physical activity as markers of masculinity, the Jews were perceived by the dominant power as passive and feminine, while Judaism developed a discourse that devalued the culture of purely muscular virility. Instead of defending themselves against these stereotypical accusations, the Jews appear to have endorsed them and reclaimed them as their own, as a way of developing anti-Roman rhetoric.[65] For the rabbis, the stereotype of this Roman masculinity is a thick brute, whereas Jewish virility appropriates other values as its own.

Numerous stories in the Talmud portray scenes where men fight with weapons other than physical strength. One could cite the example of Rabbi Yohanan ben Zakkai, the man who abandoned Jerusalem during the siege of the city by the Romans, and founded the rabbinical school of Yavneh. He is said to have pretended to be dead in order to flee the battles raging inside the walls of the sacred city during the destruction of the second Temple. In the tradition, he then came to incarnate combat through study rather than weapons. For the sake of this ideal, he was ready to humiliate himself and play dead. The Talmud makes him

65   See Daniel Boyarin, "Homotopia: The Feminized Jewish Man and the Lives of Women in Late Antiquity", *Differences*, 7/2 (1995), pp. 41–81.

the hero – not those who fought the Romans to death with their weapons, like the retrenched troops at Masada.

Another Talmudic account perfectly illustrates the confrontation of Roman manhood with the rabbinical model of virility, namely the encounter between two celebrated sages both studying at a yeshiva: Rabbi Yohanan and Reish Lakish (Babylon Talmud, Baba Metzia 84a).

The beardless scholar and the repentant gladiator: a short Talmudic study

Rabbi Yohanan and Reish Lakish lived in Palestine in the second century CE. At the start of the story about them in the Talmud, only one of them, Rabbi Yohanan, is a famous rabbi who devotes his life to study and the Torah. He is well known not only for his wisdom and erudition, but also, the Talmud tells us, for his incredible and legendary beauty. At the beginning of the story, the other character, Reish Lakish, is a Jewish brigand, whose life is very distant from the world of study. This is how their paths cross on the banks of a river: One day, Rabbi Yohanan was swimming in the Jordan River. Reish Lakish saw him and took him for a woman. He threw away his knife and plunged in after him. Rabbi Yohanan said to him: "Your strength should be devoted to Torah study." Reish Lakish replied: "And your beauty should be for women." Rabbi Yohanan then said to him: "If you change your path, I will give you my sister in marriage, who is even more beautiful than me." Reish Lakish accepted the deal. He tried to return to the shore but his strength had abandoned him. Rabbi Yohanan taught him later all the texts of the tradition and Reish Lakish became a great man.

In the waters of the Jordan, the life of the brigand Reish Lakish takes a new turn. In the middle of the river, a strange bargain is struck which is marked by a double wedding: with a woman, and with a house of study.

According to the rabbis, it is through this role of a scholar, rather than as a man of action, that true and praiseworthy virility can be expressed.

It is clear from this passage that there are two models of virility being set against each other here. On one side is Reish Lakish and a muscular, physical masculinity, influenced by the Greco-Roman world in which he lives. Physical and sexual violence are implicit in the text. A loutish brigand, the man with the knife throws himself into the water to get to the person he thinks is a woman. There, facing him, is Rabbi Yohanan, a completely different kind of man. A being of exceptional beauty, whom the Talmud describes as beardless. This detail of the Rabbi's facial hairlessness is significant. It denotes a "feminine" man, lacking the traditional attributes of masculinity. This is why he is taken to be a woman when swimming naked.

But this alternative virility is nevertheless what will prevail in combat. Reish Lakish abandons his knife, a phallic symbol, near the water. Then, as soon as he accepts Yohanan's offer, his physical strength abandons him: he has difficulty regaining the shore. It appears that a transfer of powers has taken place in the waters of the Jordan, from the muscle of a brigand to the mind of a great Talmudist.

The currency of exchange, in the deal between Yohanan and Reish Lakish, is a woman. The "real" feminine presence in the text is clearly instrumentalised, reified, in the name of the transcendent goal of bringing a man back to the Torah.

The story does not end there. One day, the two men, now inseparable study partners, friends and brothers-in-law, are debating a specific point of law, about when the fabrication of a knife is considered complete. As soon as the instrument is finished, according to law, it can be made unclean through contact with another object.

The two men set out their opposing points of view on this question, which may seem merely anecdotal: Rabbi Yohanan argues that it is the passage of the metal through fire, the moment when the object takes on its definitive form, which constitutes the point of fabrication of the knife. Reish Lakish for his part is convinced it is the passage through water, in other words scouring the metal in a liquid, which fixes the form of the object and thus seals the end stage of its fabrication. Rabbi Yohanan brings the debate to a close by telling Reish Lakish: "A bandit knows about his banditry, i.e., you are an expert in weaponry because you were a bandit in your youth." Reish Lakish, mad with rage, answers: "What benefit did you provide me by bringing me close to Torah? There, among the bandits, they called me Leader of the bandits, and here, too, they call me Leader of the bandits." Immediately after this exchange, Reish Lakish falls ill and dies. Then Rabbi Yohanan dies in turn, in despair at losing this friendship.

In the second part of the account, a battle between two men is once again described, this time transposed inside the world of the yeshiva: no longer out in nature, but in the midst of rabbinical culture. The two men fight like gladiators, not with swords or knives, but with words and arguments. Their fight is bloody and even lethal, since neither one survives the altercation.

What they are at odds over is a question of Jewish law, for such is the daily activity of the yeshiva. Debating ideas and diverging opinions of the law is an activity that, for rabbis, is elevated to a supreme value, for debate is required to interpret and to renew the reading of the texts of the law.

But in the present case, the confrontation goes badly, no doubt because the real subject of the debate is not simply the question of the status of a knife and its fabrication. What is at stake is the very nature of the relationship between these two men. A friendship that started in the waters of the Jordan ends in the discussion of issues around the immersion of an object and its purity.

The underlying question set by the debate, in my opinion, is the following: from what point onwards is something or someone finished? In other words: when can one consider the nature of an object or a living being as definitive and non-transformable? Is it the moment an object "comes out of the oven", in other words the moment of its very creation? Or is it the moment it is "plunged in water" that finalises it fabrication? The question may appear of only anecdotal importance, but Reish Lakish asks it in light of his own personal history. Is a man determined by his origins or can he, once he is immersed in the river, really change? Is there any possibility of redemption and accomplishment for him? By insisting that Reish Lakish is an expert in weaponry because he was a brigand in his youth, Rabbi Yohanan is in effect telling him: "You, the past brigand, have never ceased to be one in my eyes. You remain a stranger in the yeshiva and the world of rabbis. You will always be a Roman among us." His friend and master's arguments annihilate all hope Reish Lakish had of being recognised, of being accepted, as his study partners' equal. He confronts Rabbi Yohanan with his paradoxical thinking and tells him: the violence that was sown on the outside of the yeshiva by people like me is not that different from the violence that you sow and that reigns inside it.

In this emblematic account, it appears that the virility of rabbis is not necessarily a renunciation of the use of force, but having recourse to other weapons. Many passages in the Talmud assert in similar fashion that the words of the sages can kill.[66] Rabbinical virility is not the renunciation of force, but its transposition into words and intellect. It is this violence that finally kills Reish Lakish. The account ends without a moral, instead leaving unanswered the question that runs throughout the text from its first lines: what does "being a great man" mean? What constitutes praiseworthy and virtuous virility?

Another question remains unresolved: where are the women in this world? Are they, like the sister of Rabbi Yohanan, condemned to be only a currency of exchange, ghosts with no name or face, instrumentalised by men, or victims of their violence?

In the yeshiva, women are absent, but eroticism is not. The relationship between the two sages of the Talmud is undoubtedly platonic, and yet it is as passionate as any lovers' connection. Their closeness carries the possibility of triggering lethal emotions, like a love story that ends badly,

66 See, for example, the Talmudic treatise Yoma 87a, where a famous rabbi kills a butcher simply by standing next to him.

leading one of the protagonists to death and the other to mourning and madness. While the rabbis denounce the violence of Roman virility in this text, they are not unaware of the violence that can be generated and fuelled by their own system of values. This episode illustrates the capacity of the Talmud to generate insight into its own contradictions. The strength of this literature is often associated with its ability to foster criticism within itself, and to lay bare the paradoxes of its own world. In the same way that rabbinical culture encourages the debating of ideas and the confrontation of different points of view, the numerous accounts to which it refers tolerate the ambiguity of their messages, without dispensing simplistic moral lessons.

The Talmud is a world of men, a collection of texts edited, read and studied exclusively by men, for centuries. But a large number of them, between the lines, criticise the masculine world as a potential source of violence. Femininity in the text is reserved for the features of a wife, a sister, a child; sometimes even the features of a sage who issues a warning about the dangers of systematic exclusion, which could threaten the rabbinical enterprise and its view of the world. Discreet alterity can be found by those who seek it, in the background of masculine self-criticism. When its voice is heard at last, the text finds its modesty again. It becomes faithful again to its own values.

Not reducing women to femininity,
or men to masculinity

Femininity in the text, as we have seen, is not only incarnated by women. In the same way, being "a great man" is not reducible to the simple expression of masculinity. In other words, the Talmud appears to conceive that gender is not reducible to sex. Several texts blur the lines between the two.

Such is the case in one passage in the Talmud, which approaches this question from an original angle: what makes a man a male?

In order to understand this, it is useful to take a detour through a biblical text that may at first appear unrelated.[67] The book of Deuteronomy sets out several commandments or attitudes that are only relevant to men. It is written: "Three times a year [. . .] all your males shall appear before the Lord your God in the place that He will choose" (16:16). This verse sets out the obligation of undertaking a pilgrimage to Jerusalem three times a year. In the period of sacerdotal Judaism, when the Temple was still in Jerusalem,

67   My thanks go to Liliane Vana for pointing out this commentary, which she discussed in her January 2009 talk "Identité de genres dans la loi rabbinique" (Gender identity in rabbinical law) at the Alliance Israélite Universelle. See http://www.akadem.org/sommaire/colloques/homme-femme-question-sur-le-lien-entre-les-sexes-et-genre/identite-de-genre-selon-la-loi-rabbinique-24-07-2009-7836_4140.php.

every man was obliged to go there. This duty, which was abolished with the destruction of the Temple in the year 70 CE, applies in principle only to men.

But the Talmud deepens the analysis of this verse, and tries to understand who precisely was the addressee of this commandment, or more accurately, who was exempt:

> All are obligated in "the appearing" [i.e. making a pilgrimage on the major holidays to the Temple], except a deaf man, a mentally ill person, and a child, and one of doubtful gender [*tumtum*], and one of double gender, and women, and slaves who are not freed, the lame man, and the blind man, and the sick man, and the old man, and he who is not able to go up on his feet. [Chagiga 2a:1]

Twelve categories of people are exempt from the commandment of pilgrimage. What does this varied list tell us? The following are excluded from pilgrimage and thus from the biblical category of "male": women, but also anyone whose sex is not clearly defined (intersex person, *tumtum*), or any mentally ill person, physically disabled person or a minor.

The definition of the "male" in rabbinical literature therefore appears to be the following: an adult individual of the male sex, who is free and not disabled. From this literature's point of view, there are only two genders: male, for free (adult) men, and female, which includes anyone who is not that.

The Talmud thus envisages an original distinction between sex and gender. The male gender defines beings capable of autonomy. The female symbolically becomes the referent identity of all persons who are mentally unwell, or dependent, either physically or in terms of their status, no matter what their sex.

Maleness therefore does not pertain to all men, or at least it doesn't define them permanently. This reading might seem to be a caricature, or insulting to women, who are reduced to the gender of dependency, but in fact it gives us an important key for our analysis. Rabbinical literature considers the attributes of gender beyond the simple determination of sex: a man cannot be exclusively and permanently described as being male. If maleness does not define all men, then why should women be permanently limited by their femaleness? Talmudic literature seems much bolder in its exploration of the complexity of human identity than those who now often speak in its name.

The male is defined, in the eyes of the rabbis, as an individual who is free, and independent not only in relation to his contemporaries, but also and especially in relation to his own urges. Once again, this is affirmed by rabbinical literature in a proverb: "Who is mighty? He who subdues his [evil] inclination."[68] The real male is thus a man who has the strength to control and master his urges, to enjoy a certain autonomy in relation to his own passions. The unspoken counterpart of such a definition is a vision of the female where one of her characteristics is her dependency on her desire and submission to her inclinations.

Michael L. Satlow analyses this notion of masculinity and affirms that rabbinical Judaism defines it as a man's capacity to control his impulses; but he also reminds us that this virtue is not exclusive to Jewish discourse in antiquity.[69] This idea is also notably associated with Aristotle, who considered lack of self-control a sign of vulnerability, a characteristic that he identified as feminine.

---

68 Mishna [Pirkei] Avot 4:1, edited in the second century (*gibor* is the Hebrew word for both "mighty" and "virile").

69 Michael L. Satlow, "'Try to Be a Man': The Rabbinical Construction of Masculinity", *Harvard Theological Review*, 89/14 (1996), pp. 19–40.

The contaminating female

> The man is afraid of being weakened by the
> woman, infected with her femininity and
> of then showing himself incapable.
> Sigmund Freud, "The Taboo of Virginity"[70]

Women are often described in ancient literature as dependent beings, in relation not only to men – and particularly their husbands – but also to their own passions, whereas masculinity is defined as the gender of autonomy and self-control.

The paradox of this definition of gender is obvious.

The ultra-orthodox obsession with women's modesty demands that they hide their bodies so as not to tempt men. But why should they preserve themselves from the male gaze at all costs, when the characteristic feature of a man, of virility, is precisely the capacity to control one's own passions? Why should a woman constitute a threat to a man, when she alone is the one who is incapable of self-control? Is it about protecting her from herself, from her own urges and from her incapacity to master herself? Or is it about protecting men from an even greater threat?

According to rabbinical logic, the man who cedes to his

70 In *The Standard Edition of the Complete Psychological Works of Sigmund Freud, Vol. XI*, ed. James Strachey (London: Hogarth Press, 1910), pp. 198–9.

urges, notably his sexual passions, immediately falls into the category of the feminine.

This in fact might be the real threat: whenever a woman places a man in a situation where he might cede to temptation, she makes him run the risk of feminisation. Men therefore seek to hide women, because any contact with them involves the risk that a man might himself become a woman. Keeping women at a distance, and covered, is much the same as saying: "Thank God I'm not you!" Men see the need to protect themselves from the contamination of femininity.

CHAPTER EIGHT

Femininity as Blessing

"Thank God I'm not you": this imperative to keep women at a distance is almost the same as the words that traditionalist Jewish men recite every morning. Daily liturgy always includes the blessing "Blessed are you, Lord, our God, ruler of the universe who has not created me a woman."[71] This saying, which expresses gratitude at not belonging to the other sex, has long been removed from liberal Jewish prayer books. In the orthodox world, it is often the object of interpretations and attempts at justification that can only be described as apologetic. Many exegetes have tried to make its message "kosher" and to soften its meaning, in order to make it audible and digestible for the new generation.

A traditional example of such an argument comes from the pen of Chief Rabbi Ernest Gugenheim (1916–77), who writes that, through this blessing, "men express their

71   See Eliezer Segal, "Who Has Not Made Me a Woman", My Jewish Learning, https://www.myjewishlearning.com/article/who-has-not-made-me-a-woman.

gratitude at being subject to all the *mitzvot* (commandments), given that women are exempt from some of them".[72]

In this interpretation, what men are congratulating themselves for every morning is not what they have avoided – being female – but what they have not avoided – the religious commandments that are incumbent upon them as men. Indeed, men's duties cover a wider set of practices than women's. According to tradition, women are exempt from a number of rites, notably the use of tefillin (phylacteries) or the prayer shawl. Why is this? Because, Rabbi Gugenheim continues, a woman "doesn't really need them. As a matter of fact, she carries in the depths of her being, biologically, a disposition to sanctification. She is exempt from these commandments not because she is not worthy of them, but because she has, so to speak, a more intuitive, more direct knowledge of divinity".[73]

A similar argument comes from Rabbi Aharon Solo-veichik, who explains, for his part, that women must obey fewer commandments "because, intrinsically, they possess an inner spiritual superiority".[74]

72 In *Les Portes de la Loi. Études et Responsa* (The gates of the law, studies and responsa) (Paris: Albin Michel, 1982), cited in Ryvon Krygier, *La Loi juive à l'aube du XXIe siècle* (Jewish law at the dawn of the twenty-first century) (Paris: Biblieurope, 1999), p. 196.

73 Ibid.

74 "The Attitude of Judaism Toward the Woman", *Major Addresses Delivered at Midcontinent Conclave and National Leadership Conference, Union of Orthodox Jewish Congregations*, November 27–30, 1969 (New York: UOJC, 1970) p. 27.

What we are seeing with these kinds of justifications is a radical reversal in argumentation. What appeared in the text as a disabling status or as the essential inferiority of women is here interpreted as the expression of a superior feminine essence. Women are said not to be "defective" in comparison to Jewish men, but to be in possession of an innate privilege that exempts them from the obligation of a religious practice as rigorous as that of men. Women apparently do not need to be shaped by the rites, but benefit from a natural predisposition, an innate spiritual sophistication.

This apologetic reading is not followed unanimously in all interpretations. It is unconvincing, in that the blessing does clearly express the status of manhood as a fortunate privilege. In the two morning blessings that precede this one, men give thanks to God for having not been created a slave or a non-Jew. It is difficult to imagine how these two conditions could also present an essential or spiritual superiority in the eyes of the rabbis, when compared to that of the free Jewish man. Why, among these other forms of alterity, would being female be the only condition worthy of a positive reading?

It's either one thing or the other: either being female represents, as servitude does, a handicap that men are spared and consider themselves grateful for not having, or it represents an essential superiority, as the apologetic reading would have it. In the latter case, the man, who is naturally deprived of this "spiritual supplement", experiences the practice which allows him to acquire it as beneficial. He blesses God for not creating him a woman, in other words for not creating him as a being who is "emasculated" of the duty of practising and seeking perfection that is religious worship. In both these cases, the feminine is presented as a gender of "deficiency", where even a possible supplementary talent is seen as a form of handicap.

The origins of this prayer are unknown. Some researchers have shed light on the similarities between the blessings in the Jewish morning prayer and those from other cultures and civilisations with which the rabbis came into contact. Liliane Vana notably reminds us that "Plato thanks the Gods for being born 'human and not animal, man and not woman, Greek and not barbarian' (whereas) the faithful worshipper of Ahura Mazda expresses his thanks 'to God Hormizd for having made him Iranian and a son of the right religion and the human race, [. . .] free and not a slave, man and not woman.'"[75] This Jewish prayer might therefore be a borrowing or an adaptation of a text that did not originate in Judaism. We must now ask ourselves why it is still kept in the prayer book as is, in the name of faithfulness to an immemorial tradition, especially when alternative versions of this blessing have been written down throughout

75 Liliane Vana, "Béni soi-tu . . . qui ne m'a pas fait femme" (Blessed are you . . . who did not make me a woman), *Tsafon*, 60 (2010–11), p. 101.

Jewish history. In 1471, the Italian rabbi Abraham Farissol (1451–1525) composed a book of prayers in which a symmetrical and egalitarian blessing appears: "Blessed are you who made me a woman and not a man."[76]

The "too" deficient being

In rabbinical literature, women are described either as deficient or as excessive beings. Sometimes they are described as emotionally or religiously disabled, incapable of autonomy and control, sometimes as too intimately connected to the sacred or divinity to require a religious practice.

This paradox of "deficiency" and "excess" echoes the ambivalences in the perception of "the feminine" in psychoanalytic literature. The Freudian theory of the difference between the sexes, and of the anxiety this leads to in the individual, repeatedly insists on the mental repercussions for both sexes of a female anatomical deficiency. Freud describes female genitals, where the penis, "this part of the body, prized above all else, really is absent",[77] as triggering in men a fear of castration that would deprive them of their bodily "added extra". But, simultaneously, the anxiety that

76 Malul, Chen, "The Feminist Version of the Jewish Morning Blessing", 11 June 2017, The Librarians, https://blog.nli.org.il/en/first_feminist_siddur/.
77 *An Outline of Psychoanalysis*, tr. Helena Ragg-Kirkby (London: Penguin, 2003), p. 218.

the female body arouses is said to have something to do with its characteristic as a secreting being. Female genitals are frightening because they exude. Women are what overflows and must be contained, beings whose excessive discharge must be staunched.

A missing element or an overflowing one, the feminine is always "too" something: too empty or too full. This ambivalence in women's status places them in a position of permanent alterity with regard to men. But even beyond women's situation in relation to men, the feminine seems to constitute a kind of alterity for humankind more generally. According to Jacqueline Schaeffer, it is always "the other sex", whether one is a man or a woman.[78] It is other, in relation to a norm that remains male for all humanity, like emptiness in relation to fullness. This is also what Emmanuel Levinas expresses in *Totality and Infinity*, when he writes that the feminine is essentially the "Other", and that any relationship with it is a connection that will be forever slipping away.[79]

78 "Le fil rouge du sang de la femme" (The red thread of women's blood), *Champ psychosomatique*, 40 (2006), pp. 39–64.
79 *Totality and Infinity: An Essay on Exteriority*, tr. Alphonso Lingis (Pittsburgh: Duquesne University Press, 1969).

Gender theory

There are many feminine behaviours, in the feminine.
But I think, from the depths of my work, that this
feminine does not belong to women.
Élisabeth Badinter[80]

For many philosophers and psychoanalysts, femininity is no longer considered an exclusive attribute of women, nor as an essential characteristic of their nature or their way of being in the world. It remains an indefinable word, not reducible to a gendered identity. The refusal of a perfect and absolute symmetry between gender and sex is at the heart of what has in the last few years been called gender theory. This academic discipline, which is particularly developed in the USA and influenced by the work of French philosophers such as Michel Foucault and Jacques Derrida, explores the relations between men and women not only through the prism of sex as it is biologically defined, but also through gender as a socially constructed status. Gender theory argues that all binary systems of opposition (male/female, soul/body, pure/impure, clean/dirty . . .) express a hierarchy between these opposing terms. One of the terms

80 In Catherine Rodgers, *Le Deuxième Sexe de Simone de Beauvoir. Un héritage admiré et contesté* (The Second Sex by Simone de Beauvoir: an admired and contested heritage) (Paris: L'Harmattan, 1998), p. 69.

of the equation is accorded value, to the detriment of the other.

While numerous disciplines have long considered notions of masculinity and femininity as separate from men and women, this dichotomy is firmly rejected by traditional religious thought, which persists in making biological sex and gender identity coincide, even though, as we have explored in the preceding chapters, femininity is often appropriated by Jewish men as a part of worship, and even though the Talmud considers masculinity as only applying to some men.

In the context of the public debate about gay marriage, virulent attacks on gender theory have been launched by influential religious public figures who accuse this discipline of threatening the separation between the sexes, the order of family life and the very foundation of filiation.

The Chief Rabbi of France, Gilles Bernheim, in his essay against the proposed legalisation of same-sex marriage, specifically warned against the attempts of gender theory as well as one of its variants, queer theory, to institute "a new anthropology [. . .] with the goal of returning to a primary state where there were no sexual or gendered differences".[81] The negation of the difference between the sexes, in favour

81 "Mariage homosexual, homoparentalité, adoption: ce que l'on oublie souvent de dire" (Homosexual marriage, same-sex parenting, adoption: what we often forget to say), October 2012, Crif, http://crif.org/fr/tribune/mariage-homosexuel-homoparentalité-adoption-ce-que-lon-oublie-souvent-de-dire/33000.

of a chosen or felt gender, was similarly denounced by Pope Benedict XVI in his 2012 Christmas message to the Roman Curia, when he saluted the document composed by Gilles Bernheim at some length, taking up his arguments in order to denounce the theory that "sex is no longer a given element of nature, that man has to accept and personally make sense of: it is a social role that we choose for ourselves, while in the past it was chosen for us by society. The profound falsehood of this theory and of the anthropological revolution contained within it is obvious."[82]

These representatives of the Abrahamic religions are banding together against this philosophical theory of gender. In defining the threat that it represents, the Pope and the Chief Rabbi echo each other in reminding the faithful that it is the sexual difference between men and women, their essential dissimilarity, that constitutes the foundation of the encounter with others, the sacred alterity that is the basis of continued existence. To show the ontological complementarity of the two sexes, the Pope and the rabbi both cite the same verse from Genesis about the creation of the first man: "And God created man in His image, in the image of

82 "Address of His Holiness Benedict XVI on the Occasion of Christmas Greetings to the Roman Curia", https://www.vatican.va/content/benedict-xvi/en/speeches/2012/december/documents/hf_ben-xvi_spe_20121221_auguri-curia.html.

God He created him; *male and female* He created them" (1:27; my emphasis).

Benedict XVI and Gilles Bernheim both cite this verse, but surprisingly, both introduce a nuance that is not present in the etymological translation of the text. Both choose to translate the verse in the following way: "And God created man in His image, in the image of God He created him; *man and woman* He created them" (my emphasis).

In the original verse the Hebrew words *zakhar* and *nekeva* appear, two terms that can be translated as male and female, or masculine and feminine, but *not* as man and woman (which in Biblical Hebrew are *ish* and *isha*).

It is thus on this distorted meaning of the Bible verse that the Pope's and Chief Rabbi's common argument is based. Where the original verse suggests a complementarity in the male and female genders (which can be expressed within one person or between two individuals), the emphasis is suddenly placed on the complementarity of the sexes, man and woman, as two differentiated beings.

It is clear how the text supports their argument when translated in this way, by affirming that sexual difference and the complementarity of man and woman are at the heart of the divine plan and the very meaning of the creation of humankind.[83] This is an attempt to warn against the

83 Chief Rabbi Gilles Bernheim asserts that "Genesis sees the resemblance of human beings with God only through the association of a man and a woman

ravages of the denial of sexual difference, and of the illusion of absolute freedom of choice when it comes to our gender identities.

Gender theory, in its radical version, does in fact run the risk of monist reduction, when it proposes a world view that recognises no innate distinction between human beings, where all binary systems are abolished. Man and woman no longer exist within that world view, since they both define themselves within the hybridity of possible identities. What is the point, then, of setting out to encounter one another, when this other is already one of my component parts and already makes me a complete, self-sufficient being?

Then again, inversely, doesn't traditionalist religious discourse propose an equally reductive vision of what separates human beings and what constructs identity? Equating everyone only with their biological sex runs the risk of a considerable impoverishment of the human condition. In such a world view, masculinity belongs only to men, whereas a woman can only incarnate "womanhood", or rather "the eternal feminine".

Denying sex in favour of gender, or restricting each sex

(Genesis 1:27) and not in each of them taken separately. Which suggests that the definition of a human being is only perceptible in the conjunction of the two sexes" (ibid., p. 21).

to the values and attributes of their gender: both initiatives can equally reveal themselves to be caricatures or over-simplifications.

Numerous religious representatives are now invoking the laws of nature to justify the roles ascribed to everyone. But biology has long since ceased to consider nature as an "order" which knows no random occurrences. It has ceased to believe in the absolute genetic conditioning of human beings, in favour of epigenesis. Humankind is not simply defined by the innate data of its heritage, but also by the turns that its history, culture and environment have made its identity take. Traditional religious discourse, in its own way, grasps at the all-genetic model, where biological sex alone determines our identities as men and women.

Thinking about gender without confusion

It is essential these days to encourage a serious consideration of gender within religious traditions. This discussion, which has already started in North America, is all the more complex in that religious thinking and rituals constantly structure the world into binary and opposing states, between which humanity must find its way.

In Judaism, for example, this division of the world is omnipresent: separations are established between statuses (kosher/not kosher, pure/impure, etc.) and particularly between genders (men/women). Religious practice is suspicious of blurry and hybrid zones, and often orders the universe into distinct categories and warns against anything that might generate confusion.

The confusion of genders constitutes a primary threat, which is defined in traditional sources as an "abomination". In the Bible this term, *toevah* in Hebrew, qualifies two very specific interdicts.

The first is the prohibition of cross-dressing: "A woman must not put on man's apparel, nor shall a man wear woman's clothing; for whoever does these things is abhorrent to the Lord your God" (Deuteronomy 22:5).

The second is the famous verse from Leviticus, which is traditionally interpreted as a condemnation of masculine homosexuality: "Do not lie with a male as one lies with a woman; it is an abhorrence" (18:22).

What these two "transgressions" have in common seems to be the confusion of genders that they point to. The clear separation between masculine and feminine is disturbed.

In the Bible, confusion is synonymous with chaos. When the world appears in Genesis, each element of the Creation emerges through its distinction from another, which is then placed in opposition to it. The earth is separated from the sea, the oceans from the sky, light from darkness.

All creation is differentiated into a binary system. With the exception of one creature: man.

However, a careful reading of the beginnings of human-kind reveals a genesis of genders that is far more subtle than a simple binary. A return to the Garden of Eden will allow us to conceive of the difference between the masculine and feminine in a new way.

Return to Paradise

As we saw in our Chapter Three, the first parts of Genesis present two contradictory versions of the creation of man. Initially created "male and female", the first human is not the product of a distinction, of a clear separation. The original Adam was ontologically indistinct, or more accurately, was a mixture of genders (and not sexes).

It is only later, in the second chapter of Genesis, that the story of sexual differentiation is told to us. This time, Adam is alone in the Garden, and "he does not find a companion facing him" (Genesis 2:20). He sets out in search of a female partner, as if he was already differentiated, already completely male.

We know, however, from the first chapter of Genesis, that Adam is not completely male. The perception of his mascu-linity is therefore not the simple expression of his biological sex identity, but a reflection of his subjectivity. He wakes up as male because he is seeking a female, or because the Other has appeared before him.

Let us imagine for a moment that the two successive accounts, which may initially seem irreconcilable, are simply the reflection of two points of view of the same story. Primordial Adam is divinely constituted to begin with, with attributes that are called "male and female" (Genesis 1:27).

But he does not yet perceive this. Like the Adam of the start of Chapter Two, man, barely created, believes himself to be exclusively of one gender, the male gender in fact, which constitutes the original one in his eyes. As if femaleness, which is also part of him from the beginning, was suppressed and appeared in his world view as only secondary, off to one side. This femaleness will become visible and reveal itself to him only if man pulls himself out of his torpor, and perceives that this female side is flesh of his flesh.[84]

Shmuel Trigano reminds us that in Hebrew the word for "male" is *zakhar*, a word that literally means "to remember": the male is ontologically marked by forgetting, by the amnesia of the other gender that is part of him. He is called upon to remember what is inside him and has been ever

84 Of course, the terms "male" and "female" are to be understood more broadly than as a simple difference in sex.

since creation, in order to rehabilitate the femaleness that was obliterated or fell into a "gap in his memory".[85]

These days, traditional religious discourse seems to suffer from the same amnesia and to remain, so to speak, in the image of the first man, at the time when his female side was eclipsed. It is undoubtedly up to today's exegetes to make the feminine in the text emerge, to pull it out of the torpor into which they themselves have plunged it.

This feminine can be defined as an alterity that is there in the shadows, waiting to be revealed. It is what Jacques Derrida qualifies as "new ground whence something as yet unknown still could come, something different, other . . . *perchance*."[86]

To set out in search of the feminine does not entail denying the difference between the sexes or the foundational alterity of conjugal life. Adam is not Eve, but it is up to him to remember that, originally, he was also created female. This awareness of the complexity of identity holds the promise of an enrichment of religious thought. The dominant version of history and tradition, the male version, now needs to be awakened to its forgotten or veiled versions.

*

85 In Hebrew, the word for "female", *nekeva*, also means hole, obliteration.
86 Carole Dely, *Jacques Derrida: the "perchance" of the coming of the other-woman*, tr. Wilson Baldridge. See http://www.sens-public.org/articles/312/.

These versions do exist, and are to be found notably within the mystical tradition. In his work on the sex of souls, Charles Mopsik explores the thinking of the many Kabbalists who considered the complexity of gender beyond its limitations to the biological sex of the individual. This is notably the case with the Vilna Gaon, who in the eighteenth century affirmed that "male and female each contain male and female".[87] Other Jewish philosophers of the eighteenth century expressed even more ambitious viewpoints on the complementarity of genders and sexuality. According to Rabbi Jacob Koppel, the desire for the opposite sex comes from an ontological bisexuality: it is because men have a feminine part in them that they are attracted to women, and vice versa.[88] For this Kabbalist and many others, it is therefore not original alterity that creates desire, but on the contrary the partial similarity of human beings of complex gender. The existence of the opposite sex within oneself is what generates the attraction to the other. Humans are therefore said to be attracted to what is similar to them, rather than to their opposite.

One can understand how these theories were later erased or obstructed by institutional authorities who were

87   In Liqoutim sur le sifra distsniouta (Likutim on the Siphra Dtzenioutha), 1873, cited in Mopsik, op. cit., p. 23.
88   Jacob Koppel, Chaarey Gan Eden, Koretz 1803, fol. 63a, cited in Mopsik, op. cit., p. 33.

concerned with controlling doctrinal truth and imposing a normative model: "Social censorship of these currents in their own communities of origin, the more or less voluntary forgetting of the contents of their discourse in the 'catechism' of orthodox Judaism, constitutes in itself an object of study. But it is beyond a doubt that they were, and are, perceived as sufficiently subversive to require this mostly silent eviction."[89]

The re-emergence of these stifled voices is now critical: not in order to instrumentalise them for political ends or a social agenda, but because we need to accept that they are also part of the corpus of religious literature that constitutes our heritage, and are therefore also "traditional". Their bold and original view could provide new food for thought regarding the place of the two genders (and not simply the two sexes) in religious thought.

The emergence of the feminine in religion will not occur through women, because the feminine does not belong to them. But it will not happen without them either. It will not occur until the voices that have until now been silenced take part in reading, commentary and debate, and until humankind can perceive the blessing of being created man or woman, male and female.

89 Ibid., p. 46.

CHAPTER NINE

Subversion

"Yes, we do offer Talmud studies, but . . . not for you." Such was the welcome I was often given a decade ago when I was knocking at the doors of study centres, seeking a place that would allow me to study the writings of our tradition. I sometimes perceived something like embarrassment in the voices of my interlocutors, and almost always surprise. There was obviously something incongruous and impertinent in my request. Was I trying to enter a world that was not mine, a world where there was no place for women?

When those doors closed, I often thought about the woman who is said to have easily fooled them, the one whose name and story are strangely stifled by our tradition: Beruriah.

A heroine in the Talmud, Beruriah is one of the very rare women to be cited there under her own name. Her father and her husband were celebrated sages, and yet the text does not make her merely a "daughter of" or "wife of". Through several accounts, she acquires a name and an exceptional story of her own.

"Berurya, wife of Rabbi Meir and daughter of Rabbi Hananya ben Teradyon, was so sharp and had such a good memory that she learned three hundred halakhot [lessons] in one day from three hundred Sages" (Babylon Talmud, Pesachim 62b).

The Talmud tells of how this erudite woman surpassed all the men around her in sagacity, knowledge and capacity for learning. She brings closure to several legal debates in the Talmud with her opinion, and her point of view is considered by sages in various circumstances to be more accurate than that of her interlocutors. Beruriah undoubtedly studied with men, debated with them and shared her erudition with them. She appeared to master the source texts, including those that were most negative towards women. With great poise and a sense of humour, she was capable of turning the most misogynistic rabbinical arguments against men.

There is a proverb that is well known among Talmud scholars: "Engage not in too much conversation with women" (Mishna Avot 1:5). The Talmud tells the story of how Beruriah was walking one day when she met a celebrated sage of the time, Rabbi Yosei of Galilee. He stopped her to ask the way: "On which path shall we walk in order to get to Lod? She said to him: Foolish Galilean, didn't the Sages say: Do not talk much with women? You should have said your question more succinctly: Which way to Lod?" (Eruvin 53b).

Beruriah has the audacity and intelligence to teach a lesson to one of the great sages of her time: if conversation with women is so useless, why should he need it? Beruriah is the woman of the Talmud who flings the inconsistencies of the text back in men's faces, and seems to ask them: are you sure you have studied well? Are you sure you really understand?

While Beruriah is an exceptional woman, her presence in the text does not necessarily mean that she actually lived. Was there really such an erudite woman in the second century CE? Did other women study alongside men? If that was the case, why does the Talmud not mention any other women?

If Beruriah is merely a literary myth, a pure invention by the rabbis, what are they trying to prove by telling us about her life? Why should an erudite woman be included in the text?

This question has no doubt troubled the generations of commentators, to the point of requiring the later addition of a dramatic denouement to the life of Beruriah. For while the Babylon Talmud, edited before the sixth century CE, praises this woman as a sage among sages, this cannot be said of medieval literature.

Five centuries after the publication of the Babylon Talmud, the most famous exegete in Jewish history, Rashi, composed a commentary on the Talmud from his vineyard in the Champagne region. This is what he has to say about Beruriah:

> One time, she mocked that which the Sages said (Kiddushin 80b), 'The conviction of women is weak about them.' And he said [to himself], 'By your life, in the end you will concede to their words.' And [so] he commanded one of his students to test her with a matter of sin. And [that student] pleaded with her many days until she agreed. And when she found out, she strangled herself.[90]

This, according to Rashi, is how Beruriah met her tragic end. Because she mocks one of the misogynistic passages of the Talmud, her husband sets her a test, which she fails. Seduced by her own husband's student, she ends up confirming the proverb she was mocking, and once her adultery is made public she has no other choice but suicide.

Beruriah's tragedy mysteriously comes to light only in the medieval era. Rashi cites this account without ever giving its source. Where did he get it from? Is it part of oral tradition, or simply the fruit of his imagination? No matter its origin, this legend remains for ever attached to the character of Beruriah. The erudite woman of the Talmud is

90 Commentary by Rashi on the treatise Avoda Zarah 18b:4.

also the one who, through her arrogance, is led astray and consequently dies. Her sin is not insignificant: it is a sexual transgression. The woman of the mind falls because of her body. This is presented as the risk that women run when they undertake study.

Once again, we need to question the historical accuracy of this account. If a woman named Beruriah had met this tragic end, why did it take five centuries for her story to be told to us? If she is only a figure in a literary myth, why does the woman who was praised in the sixth century become the one to be eliminated in the eleventh? In other words, did Beruriah kill herself, or was she assassinated because she had become an embarrassing witness?

Tolerated for a while, her presence was perhaps not so welcome in the medieval era, at the precise time when the Jewish and Christian religious texts gave women such a bad reputation.[91] Beruriah had to die on the altar of the transgressive feminine to shore up masculine hegemony.

But she is not really dead. She still has her place in the Talmud. She is one of those shades that question the text and criticise it from the inside, asking the same questions she has always asked: are you sure you have properly studied your texts? Are you certain you have understood them?

Her character, like a piece of grit in the workings of the

91 In the eleventh century, as part of the Gregorian reforms of the Church, women were excluded from many religious functions, and from universities.

machine of Talmudic exegesis, is one of what Daniel Boyarin often calls the "fissures in the text". Beruriah is the woman whose discordant voice resounds in the heart of the system of masculine hegemony and exclusion of women. Where the rabbinical norm says that no woman can study alongside men, here she is offering a respected counter-example.

Whereas Rashi attempts to eradicate the threat, the Talmud tolerates this flaw. A character like Beruriah would have been easy to erase from the text. A scribe could easily have got rid of her, made her anonymous or made her disappear into the ocean of esoteric legends. And yet she remains there, at her post, almost a symbol of reproach, a kind of Talmudic bad conscience.

We should salute the courage of those men who ensured that dissonant voices endured in the text, at the very time when other religious authorities were purging their sources or their dogmas of all traces of "heresy".

The strength of rabbinical literature is perhaps that it finds it difficult to rid itself of its grit, the grains of sand from the sediment of its past. Betraying an unwillingness to censor itself, or a wish to keep the traces of all its voices, the Talmud frequently cites the arguments of its own self-criticism and the elements of its internal questioning.

*

This has a lot to do with the culture of divergence that reigns within it. Debating ideas is held up as a supreme value, whereas consensus is not. All closed-off debate is akin to a form of heresy. This culture of discordant voices can more easily tolerate fissures in the text than a spirit of consistency.

Subversion versus perversion

The characteristic feature of fundamentalist religious discourse is to start sentences with "My tradition says that . . ." or "My scriptures state unequivocally that . . ." Whether in the Jewish tradition or that of the Koran or the Gospels, these sentences are usually followed by a unilateral declaration, a judgement with no possible moderation. The person is thus asserting that their tradition has the capacity to express itself in a unified, univocal voice on whatever subject is at hand. But is there such a thing as a monolithic tradition? Can a text be inherited and passed down from one generation to the next in way that is not equivocal? Religious systems are always composite, whether or not they are open about this, or claim it as a quality, or suppress it.

All traditions harbour minority discourses and underground voices. Each narrative carries (or hides) alternative versions, or veiled ones. These versions, which defy or question established norms, are just as traditional as the dominant or authorised versions. They exist just as legitimately, despite their lack of visibility. They constitute "sub-versions", teasing the official face, underneath the surface, like a palimpsest that reveals itself to anyone who scratches at the written surface.

These subversive writings, these fissures in the text must now fuel religious discourse and generate its self-criticism. They provide a pathway out of monolithic religious thinking, the antidote to its sclerosis. Such voices of subversion are perhaps the best ramparts against the perversion of an impudent and immodest fundamentalist discourse of which we are so often the witnesses or victims.

"How Can You Still Believe in God?"

I have lost count of how many times I have been asked this question. I think I must have often tried to explain to whoever has asked it that I don't believe in the God that they don't believe in either. That iconic figure, omniscient and interventionist, which I am supposed to love, that character who is part Father Christmas and part bogeyman, is just as distasteful to me as it is to anyone else. My religion is not a renunciation of logic or doubt. On the contrary, it is richer because of both, which appear throughout the scriptures. If I manage to get through this interrogation, then a subsidiary question always arises, which legitimately follows the first one and is specifically addressed to me as a woman-rabbi: isn't the patriarchal heritage of religion essentially misogynistic?

This simple question requires a complex answer. Anyone can easily find a series of texts, Bible verses and rabbinical interpretations from different time periods that clearly show the scant consideration the rabbis gave to the "weaker sex". But it is just as simple to argue that, from one generation to the next, a genuine concern with the female condition and the status of women was at the heart of Judaism.

Individual Bible verses or religious texts taken out of context can often make the scriptures say one thing and then its opposite.

Any answer must be contextualised. To claim that an exegete of the sixth or twelfth century is a misogynist, without taking into account the state of the society in which he lived, is to judge him in the light of modern culture and thinking. Such an approach is at best anachronistic, at worst intellectually dishonest.

The real question is not so much whether Judaism (or religion in general) is misogynistic or whether it was so in the past, in the voices of its masters such as Maimonides, Rashi or others. It is to ask whether, in the voices of its contemporary interpreters and religious representatives, it still is today.

All too often the answer to this question is affirmative. Yes, Judaism, like other religious traditions, is misogynistic when it doesn't address the question of the place of the feminine in its system of thought, when it reads texts about women, whether in the Talmud or rabbinical literature, in a way that resolutely takes no account of history, without ever taking the contexts of their readings and interpretations into consideration. It is misogynistic when it cannot conceive of a place for a woman that is not determined by her body, her reproductive functions or the attributes of her gender, when it closes the doors of houses of study and exegesis, when it chooses not to respond to the distress of women oppressed by patriarchal religious law.

While not all sources are misogynistic, it is clear that many of their interpreters are. However, the sum of their readings does not summarise the texts. What the texts can say always goes beyond what people make them say.

At the heart of the Jewish tradition are also forces of questioning, self-criticism and regeneration that deserve to be reclaimed, saluted and taught. It is up to us to make them emerge from the text, and to incarnate them in our own way. That will require us to awaken some of the voices sleeping in the text, and sometimes to create new pathways of interpretation and new ways of reading.

But isn't learning to reread at the heart of all religious endeavour? This is borne out by etymology at least. We owe to Cicero the very first appearance of the word "religious". In his *De Natura Deorum* (II, 71–2), he defines the term in this manner: "Persons who spent whole days in prayer and sacrifice to ensure that their children should outlive them were termed 'superstitious' (from *superstes*, a survivor), and the word later acquired a wider application. Those on the other hand who carefully reviewed and so to speak retraced all the lore of ritual were called 'religious' from *relegere* (to retrace or re-read)."[92]

True religion is opposed to superstition and not to rationalism. It is the skill of rereading, which invites us to revisit our texts in order to offer new prisms through which we can read them, and to refuse to fix their meaning once and for all.

What a contradiction it is then, that among the Abrahamic religions, those who now claim to be the only legitimate readers of their religious sources should be precisely those who refuse to undertake any kind of rereading of them. Religion is being usurped by "textolators",[93] those simple "readers" who cannot claim to be part of a religion in the purest sense of the word, since they have fixed the reading of their texts. Their refusal to revisit their heritage is often almost a kind of superstition: they pray not only for their children to survive them, but also that the past interpretations of the text should never die.

Those who claim to be religious have thus often already ceased to be religious. But in our society, where the term is now despised, no one would challenge them. The word

92 I wish to thank Fabrice Hadjadj for letting me know about this source. See Cicero, *De Natura Deorum*, tr. H. Rackham (Cambridge, MA: Loeb Classical Library, 1933), p. 193.

93 The French term, *textolâtre*, was coined by Marc-Alain Ouaknin.

"religion" has often become synonymous with magical thinking or puerile dogma. It rhymes with unconditional submission, obscurantism and irrationality. And it underpins fundamentalist rhetoric, which increasingly promotes and incarnates these three dispositions.

A heritage that is no longer questioned dies. Examining the sources and the rites, far from any dogmatism, is perhaps what constitutes true religion. The renewed meaning of a text that is constantly revisited is its only faithful reading. That is something I can believe in.

Feminist and Jewish, Not a Jewish Feminist

*In memory of Ariane Uzan, who when asking me
whether I really believed in all this, invited me to
leave some space for doubt, always . . .*

Two Jews are chatting outside the public bathhouse.
    One asks the other: "Did you take a bath?"
    The other replies: "No, why? Was there one missing?"[94]

Jewish wisdom enjoins us to always try to begin any speech
with a joke – what in Aramaic is called *mila debdih'uta*,
a "word of humour" – which is meant to open the mind
of the person one is addressing. This is perhaps one of the
raisons d'être of Jewish humour, which is so fascinating
and hard to define. This humour often rests on the possibility of making laughter rise up from the gaps in between
meanings: wordplay opens a crack in language, from which
laughter can burst forth. Because a word can always mean

94 This joke was told to me by Rabbi Marc-Alain Ouaknin.

more than it appears to mean, because there is always something beyond the one-way street of a single meaning, which allows for the possibility of interpretation, humour has the capacity to set our intelligence to work. The person listening has a power that is not available to the one speaking, for they have the privilege of hearing the words differently.

When the book that you are holding first appeared in 2013, and I was given the opportunity of presenting it at public lectures and discussions, I had the very strange experience of this phenomenon. I've lost count of the number of times that the person inviting me to speak made all the listeners laugh by innocently declaring, "Delphine Horvilleur will present her book *In Eve's Attire*." Italics being inaudible, there were many in the audience who heard this sentence as, perhaps, a comical promise of a somewhat unusual presentation by the author. And so much the better, because, in a way, this is exactly the kind of misunderstanding that this book is about: the fact that women are always perceived as slightly more naked than men when they speak in public, or when they simply appear in public.

Religious traditions have often considered women only as this essential nakedness or, more precisely, have made women into "uncovered" beings: even when a woman is as fully clothed as a man, she remains a little more naked than he. The hair, the face and the voice, those sites of *logos* and expression in the male subject, become, in the female, erogenous zones, indecent exposure or an intolerable temptation that must be covered. Women are actually in Eve's attire as soon as they appear outside, in the public space. The fundamentalist voices of all religions are wont to enclose this "eternal feminine" within itself, to essentialise it by associating it exclusively with one domain: the sphere of interiority, of the home, of mystery and the veil.

This view of femininity is not confined to the religious imagination: it can be found in many folk tales and legends. The heroines of our childhood stories are often like the Little Mermaid, whose song threatens men, and who is restricted to swimming only in deep water and must avoid all contact with solid ground or the outside world. She can only gain access to it on the condition of renouncing her voice and her body. In folk tales, as in religious stories, women's words are immodest: they arouse desire and disturb the order of the world. Rare are the princesses that seek adventure outside the walls of their castle or the heights of their towers without sowing chaos in the story or in nature.

The eclipsed feminine is praised and reinforced by many religions, which make women into beings that are talked about but not talked with, subjects of discussion but never a subject taking part *in* the discussion. The feminine is the gender of the Other, and of modesty. This is why it is kept at the periphery of the system, at a distance from worship, away from the rites and far from religious leadership, whose norms remain masculine.

In order to justify exclusion of this sort, apologetic arguments blossom within the three monotheistic religions. They all claim that women are so spiritual, so sensitive, so empathetic or so naturally superior to men that they should be exempt from certain commandments or tasks, that they should not be subject to the injunctions of the traditions, the weight of leadership or the heavy responsibility of religious office. They are supposed to be "above all that". This modus operandi is well known: you celebrate the feminine in order to alienate it all the more, like the elegant prelude to imprisonment in a predetermined role, assigned to women by their gender.

It is disturbing that such attitudes are sometimes held by women themselves. They sometimes stake their claim to this attributed territory all the more fiercely, as a restricted place where they can fully exercise their natural expertise. It is frequently the case that women become the most tenacious "guardians of the Temple", including of the rites that are incontestably freighted with the patriarchal agenda. They themselves are sometimes the ones who demand to be kept at a distance, or who perceive their own bodies as impure or threatening to men. Can this be understood in any way other than as a retrenched position, a default setting of unquestioning religious commitment? For want of free access to the texts and their interpretation, to the knowledge and exegesis that is the foundation of all religious power, they can only defend what comes to them "filtered" through the all-masculine interpretation of the texts, and establish themselves as the keepers and protectors of the permanence of these readings.

Without access to the texts or to knowledge, no critical reading of a religious heritage is possible. The only possible link to it is through the reinforcement of existing traditions, with no opportunity to revisit or re-examine them. Access to knowledge and exegesis of the texts incontestably remains the key to women's real emancipation in the religious world. For it is only thanks to this access that we can give back to the scriptures their power of expression, and not restrict them to repeating what they have been saying for centuries. The possibility of critical readings depends on it.

A particularly famous example of the rereading of a text is presented in this book, with the account in Genesis of the creation of Eve from Adam's "rib". The Hebrew uses a term that, almost everywhere else in the sources, means "side" and not "rib". Knowing this, does the woman in the text appear as a bone, in other words a supporting element subordinate to a primary masculine being, or is she "beside" Adam, in the first face-to-face encounter in history? This double meaning in Hebrew invites us to ask ourselves what might have been the outcome, had the translation that has been imposed for centuries not been the one that prevailed.

But what are we really saying, when we affirm that the text could have been read and interpreted differently?

In my view, it would be an error to suggest that past readings are all faulty and that new traditions are needed to correct them. That would be saying that the text is always more "feminist" than its readers, or that the men who interpret it are always more "misogynistic" than is the text. Besides the fact that these categories are anachronistic and inadequately describe the readers who came before us, and who belonged to a completely different cultural universe, this defence of the text "at any cost" against what people have made it say leads us into the pitfalls of an apologetic approach. This would amount to claiming that the text can only conform itself to our own sensibilities or culture. As if we needed to save the honour of a verse, or even of God himself, by preserving it from readings that are illegitimate or immoral in our eyes. *The question is never so much what the text means, but what we do with whatever we make it mean.* The woman created by Adam's side has been obliged to live through the centuries bearing that "rib" as others have borne their cross (if I may be allowed this allegorical borrowing). And even today, female identity continues to inherit that reading.

It therefore seems to me that it is more pertinent to recognise that this text has been interpreted according to that reading for centuries, and that we are the children of that reading, whether we like it or not. But because we know that there are other possible meanings, and because we are also the children of a context that allows us to practise critical readings and to rethink the relations between the sexes, we are allowed to enrich and fertilise our relationship with the text through more complex rereadings.

It is thus up to us to continue to make the text speak, a text that is neither feminist nor misogynistic, but is simply there, haunted by what it has been made to say, but also ready to say more, through us. And its sacredness derives from the fact that it never ceases to "make sense", and is always waiting for new readers to make it speak again. Our scriptures have not finished saying what they have to say, unless our ideology gags them and uses them as a pretext for shoring up our own certainties.

It is for this reason, in my opinion, that there is a misunderstanding about so-called "religious" feminism, whether it is Jewish, Christian or Muslim. At a time when some people are suggesting that it is simply enough for a woman of religion to speak for her words to be "feminist", it seems important to remember what feminism is, whether it is voiced by a man or a woman: namely, critical thinking that opposes a system which alienates the feminine, a universal engagement that tolerates no other qualification. It is incontestable that traditional exegeses of our scriptures have served, or contributed to, the alienation of women throughout history and that they continue to do this in many places today, and this is why I see it as impossible to speak of "religious feminism". We must strive to keep our traditions alive and pertinent, by allowing them to be studied by erudite feminist women and men. We must ask ourselves how they might then live up to their ideals of justice and equality, thanks to future men and women who read their verses.

This is why I am not a Jewish feminist, but feminist and Jewish. Because I believe that my feminist activism will find a way to enrich this Jewish reading of the texts that are the foundation of my religious identity. Nothing is more immodest than to undress a text of the meanings it might yet have.

Paris, October 24, 2017.

Bibliography

Austin, J. L., *How To Do Things With Words* (Oxford: Clarendon Press, 1962).

Barthes, Roland, *The Pleasure of the Text*, tr. Richard Millar (New York: Farrar, Straus and Giroux, 1975).

Bebe, Pauline, *Isha. Dictionnaire des femmes et du judaïsme* (Isha: a dictionary of women and Judaism) (Paris: Calmann-Lévy, 2001).

Benslama, Fethi, "Le Sexuel monothéiste et sa traduction scientifique" (Monotheistic sexuality and its scientific translations), *Cliniques Méditerranéennes*, 73 (2006), pp. 89–95.

Benslama, Fethi, "Le voile de l'Islam" (The veil of Islam), *Contretemps*, 2/3 (1997), pp. 99–111.

Bernheim, Gilles, "Mariage homosexual, homoparentalité, adoption: ce que l'on oublie souvent de dire" (Homosexual marriage, same-sex parenting, adoption: what we often forget to say), October 2012, Crif, http://crip.org/fr/tribune/mariage-homosexuel-homoparentalité-adoption-ce-que-lon-oublie-souvent-de-dire/33000.

Boyarin, Daniel, "'This We Know to Be the Carnal Israel': Circumcision and the Erotic Life of God and Israel", *Critical Inquiry*, 18 (1992), pp. 474–505.

Boyarin, Daniel, *Carnal Israel: Reading Sex in Talmudic Culture* (Berkeley, CA: University of California Press, 1993).

Boyarin, Daniel, "Jewish Masochism: Couvade, Castration and Rabbis in Pain", *American Imago*, 51 (1994), pp. 3–36.

Boyarin, Daniel, "Homotopia: The Feminized Jewish Man and the Lives of Women in Late Antiquity", *Differences*, 7/2 (1995), pp. 41–81.

Boyarin, Daniel, *Unheroic Conduct: The Rise of Heterosexuality and the Invention of the Jewish Man* (Berkeley, CA: University of California Press, 1997).

Cicero, *De Natura Deorum*, tr. H. Rackham (Cambridge, MA: Loeb Classical Library, 1933).

Cixous, Hélène and Jacques Derrida, *Veils*, tr. Geoffrey Bennington (Stanford, CA: Stanford University Press, 2001).

Dely, Carole, *Jacques Derrida: The "Perchance" of the Coming of the Otherwoman*, tr. Wilson Baldridge, http://www.sens-public.org/articles/312/.

Douglas, Mary, *Purity and Danger: An Analysis of Concepts of Pollution and Taboo* (London: Routledge, 1966).

"Dr. Laura and Leviticus", *America*, August 18, 2020, https://www.americamagazine.org/faith/2010/08/18/dr-laura-and-leviticus.

Eilberg-Schwartz, Howard, *God's Phallus and Other Problems for Men and Monotheism* (Boston, MA: Beacon Press, 1994).

Eilberg-Schwartz, Howard and Wendy Doninger, *Off With Her Head! The Denial of Women's Identity in Myth, Religion, and Culture* (Berkeley, CA: University of California Press, 1995).

Eisenstein, J. D., ed., *Otzar Midrashim* (New York: J. D. Eisenstein, 1915).

Epstein, Louis M., *Sex Laws and Customs in Judaism* (Hoboken, NJ: Ktav Publishing House, 1968).

Freud, Sigmund, *The Standard Edition of the Complete Psychological Works of Sigmund Freud, Vol. XI*, ed. James Strachey (London: Hogarth Press, 1910).

Freud, Sigmund, *The Standard Edition of the Complete Psychological Works of Sigmund Freud, Vol. XXI*, ed. James Strachey (London: Vintage, 2001).

Freud, Sigmund, *An Outline of Psychoanalysis*, tr. Helena Ragg-Kirkby (London: Penguin, 2003).

Freud, Sigmund and Joseph Breuer, *Studies in Hysteria*, tr. Nicola Luckhurst (London: Penguin, 2004).

Gilman, Sander L., *Jewish Self-Hatred: Antisemitism and the Hidden Language of the Jews* (Baltimore, MD: Johns Hopkins University Press, 1986).

Gilman, Sander L., *The Jew's Body* (New York & London: Routledge, 1992).

Greenberg, Steven, *Wrestling With God and Men: Homosexuality in the Jewish Tradition* (Madison, WI: University of Wisconsin Press, 2004).

Horvilleur, D., E. Papernik and D. Muskat, "Manteau de protection, manteau de vulnérabilité" (Coat of protection, coat of vulnerability), *Tenou'a*, 147.

Iacub, Marcela, *Par le Trou de la serrure. Une histoire de la pudeur publique* (Through the keyhole: a history of public modesty) (Paris: Fayard, 2008).

Kogan, Ilany, *Escape from Selfhood: Breaking Boundaries and Craving for Oneness* (London: Routledge, 2007).

Kosman, Admiel, *Men's Tractate: Rav and the Butcher and Other Stories – On Manhood, Love and Authentic Life in Aggadic and Hassidic Stories* (in Hebrew) (Jerusalem: Keter, 2002).

Krygier, Rivon, *La Loi juive à l'aube du XXIe siècle* (Jewish law at the dawn of the twenty-first century) (Paris: Biblieurope, 1999).

Levinas, Emmanuel, *Totality and Infinity: An Essay on Morality*, tr. Alphonso Lingis (Pittsburgh: Duquesne University Press, 1969).

Lévi-Strauss, Claude, *The Elementary Structures of Kinship*, tr. James Harle Bell, John Richard von Sturmer and Rodney Needham (Boston, MA: Beacon Press, 1969).

Malul, Chen, "The Feminist Version of the Jewish Morning Blessing", 11 June 2017, The Librarians, https://blog.nli.org.il/en/first_feminist_siddur/.

Masson, Céline, ed., *Shmattès. La mémoire par le rebut* (Shmattès: memory from scraps) (Limoges: Éditions Lambert-Lucas, 2007).

Mopsik, Charles, *Sex of the Soul: The Vicissitudes of Sexual Difference in Kabbalah* (Los Angeles: Cherub Press, 2005).

Morali, Giles-Avraham, *Kabbale, corps et âme* (Kabballah, body and soul) (Villeurbanne: Éditions Ramhal, 2009).

Morel Cinq-Mars, José, *Quand la pudeur prend corps* (When modesty takes on a body) (Paris: Le Monde-PUF, 2002).

Nietzsche, Friedrich, *The Joyous Science*, tr. and ed. R. Kevin Hill (London: Penguin Classics, 2018).

Ouaknin, Marc-Alain, *The Burnt Book: Reading the Talmud* (Princeton, NJ: Princeton University Press, 1998).

Ouaknin, Marc-Alain, *Zeugma: Mémoire biblique et déluges contemporains* (Zeugma: biblical memory and contemporary deluges) (Paris: Le Seuil, 2008).

Perrault, Charles, *The Fairy Tales of Charles Perrault*, tr. Robert Samber and J. E. Mansion (London: Harrap, 1922).

Philo, *Philo* Volume IX, tr. F. H. Colson, Loeb Classical Library 363 (Cambridge, MA: Harvard University Press, 1941).

Pope Benedict XVI, "Address of His Holiness Benedict XVI on the Occasion of Christmas Greetings to the Roman Curia", https://www.vatican.va/content/benedict-xvi/en/speeches/2012/december/documents/hf_ben-xvi_spe_20121221_auguri-curia.html.

Proust, Marcel, *In Search of Lost Time, Vol. 6: Time Regained*, tr. Andreas Mayor and Terence Kilmartin, rev. D. J. Enright (New York: Modern Library, 1981).

Rodgers, Catherine, *Le Deuxième Sexe de Simone de Beauvoir. Un heritage admiré et contesté* (Simone de Beauvoir's *The Second Sex*: an admired and contested heritage) (Paris: L'Harmattan, 1998).

Sanchez-Cardenas, Michel, *"La pudeur, un lieu de liberté?* de Monique Selz" (Modesty, a space of freedom? by Monique Selz), *Revue française de psychanalyse*, 68 (2004), pp. 699–702.

Satlow, Michael L., "'Try to Be a Man': The Rabbinical Construction of Masculinity", *Harvard Theological Review*, 89/14 (1996), pp. 19–40.

Schaeffer, Jacqueline, "Le fil rouge du sang de la femme" (The red thread of women's blood), *Champ psychosomatique*, 40 (2006).

Segal, Eliezer, "Who Has Not Made Me a Woman", My Jewish Learning, https://www.myjewishlearning.com/article/who-has-not-made-me-a-woman.

"Sexualité féminine et judaïsme – Se préparer à l'intimité", Ecoute juive, www.ecoute-juive.com/nidah-sexualite-et-plaisir-femme-et-thora.php.

Singer, Isaac Bashevis, "Yentl the Yeshiva Boy", *The Collected Stories of Isaac Bashevis Singer*, tr. Marion Magid and Elizabeth Pollet (London: Jonathan Cape, 1982).

"Le silence des rabbins" (The silence of the rabbis), *Les Dernières Nouvelles d'Alsace*, 11 January 2012,https://www.dna.fr/religions/2012/01/11/le-silence-des-rabbins.

Soloveichik, Aharon, "The Attitude of Judaism Toward the Woman", *Major Addresses Delivered at Midcontinent Conclave and National Leadership Conference, Union of Orthodox Jewish Congregations*, November 27–30, 1969 (New York: UOJC, 1970) pp. 21–32.

Tisseron, Serge, *La Honte: Psychanalyse d'un lien social* (Shame: psychoanalysis of a social bond) (Paris: Dunod "Psychismes", 1992).

Tisseron, Serge, *L'Intimité surexposée* (Overexposed intimacy) (Paris: Ramsay, 2001).

Trigano, Shmuel, *Le Judaïsme et l'esprit du monde* (Judaism and the spirit of the world) (Paris: Grasset, 2012).

Vana, Liliane, "Béni soi-tu . . . qui ne m'a pas fait femme" (Blessed are you . . . who did not make me a woman), *Tsafon*, 60 (2010–11).

Wiesel, Elie, *Messengers of God: Biblical Portraits and Legends*, tr. Marion Wiesel (New York: Random House, 1976).

Zagdanski, Stéphane, *L'Impureté de Dieu* (The impurity of God) (Paris: Éditions du Félin, 1991).

Acknowledgements

I wish to thank the students of the Biblical Café, the interactive study circle of the MJLF (Liberal Jewish Movement of France), who shared their voices with the text and gave birth to the project of this book. My thanks to Paul Bernard, Jennifer Schwartz and Antoine Strobel-Dahan for their precious advice and comments.

Finally, thanks to Ariel, who knows so well how to be *"a fitting helper"* for me (Genesis 2:18).

DELPHINE HORVILLEUR is one of the few female rabbis in France. She studied at the Hebrew University of Jerusalem and worked as a journalist on French television for three years before moving to New York and beginning her rabbinical studies. She was ordained in 2008 and belongs to the Mouvement juif libéral de France. She drew media attention in the wake of the rise of antisemitic attacks and vandalism in France for her consistently compelling case for laicity and her strong feminist stance on social justice issues. She has written for the *Washington Post* and *Haaretz*. She is the author of four books, including *Anti-Semitism Revisited*, which was published English in 2021.

RUTH DIVER is a New Zealand literary translator and a former lecturer in Comparative Literature at the University of Auckland. Her translation of *Street Rounds in Paris* by Sophie Pujas won the 2016 Asymptote Close Approximations Fiction Prize. She has translated works by several of France's leading contemporary novelists, including *The Little Girl on the Ice Floe* by Adélaide Bon and *The Revolt* by Clara Dupont-Monod.